BIOGRAPHIES A
New l
INDIANS

Illustration by Robert J. Neary

CONTENTS

PREFACE

King Philip's flight into Nipmuck Country was slowed considerably by the heavy burdens his people were carrying. This was the first time in Pokanoket history they had been forced to abandon the villages in the Mount Hope peninsula that for the past 68 years had served as the seat of government for the Wampanoag Federation, and it was only natural that a vast amount of tribal memorabilia had accumulated in that time. Along with the personal effects of each family, these created such a problem in transportation that even the younger children were forced to carry heavy packs. Had the English soldiers and their Mohican allies caught up with them, it is possible that Philip would have surrendered without putting up even a token struggle in order to protect the women and children. If this had happened, the other New England tribes would in all probability have abandoned their fight for freedom, and the ensuing months of terror, destruction, and mass killing would have been avoided.

That Philip managed to escape at all was due partly to the ineptness of the English military leaders, and partly to the bravery of Woonasham, a high-ranking member of the Wampanoag Council, who, with the help of a small band of select warriors, gallantly fought a delaying action against the numerically superior English forces to give the main body of Indians time in which to reach the relative security of Nipmuck Country. Woonasham and 13 of his men were killed in the brief skirmish that followed, and their deaths left Philip in an extremely vulnerable position. When he learned that his rear guard had been destroyed, Philip ordered his people to rid themselves of all those possessions that were not immediately needed for their survival. Although this allowed them to move ahead at a much more rapid pace, he knew that the fleet-footed Mohicans could easily overtake them, and he stoically waited for his old enemies to attack.

That the expected attack did not materialize was due to the greed of the Mohicans, who stopped their pursuit to plunder the stores dropped by the fleeing Wampanoags. When the soldiers saw they had been abandoned by their Indian allies, they refused to continue the chase, stating that the extreme heat had sapped them of so much strength they could go no farther. The leaders made no effort to assert their authority, and only after Captain Daniel Henchman arrived was a semblance of discipline restored. When the soldiers were again ready to resume the chase, Philip was already in Nipmuck Country, and Henchman dismissed the Mohicans, then returned to Boston.

Once Philip was certain that the English had turned back, he sent most of his old men, women and children to Ninigret, Sachem of the Eastern Niantics, where he hoped they would be cared for until the war was over. He then continued on toward the Connecticut River, arriving at Hatfield on August 5, at which time he was greeted by a force of Nipmucks who had just returned from a raid at Brookfield.

SAKONNET RELATIONS WITH THE ENGLISH

Included among those who accompanied King Philip were warriors from almost every tribe in southern New England. For the most part, these were young men, for too many of the leaders and the other men did not rally to the common cause as enthusiastically as might be expected. There were even those, notably the Mohicans of Connecticut, who allied themselves with the English as soon as the war began. Uncas, Great Sachem of the Mohican Federation, made no secret of the fact that he hoped to someday become the most powerful Indian leader in New England, and he saw that the war could be the vehicle to fulfill his long-awaited ambition.

Also, many of those Indians who had been converted to Christianity and who lived in so-called Praying Indian towns on land granted them by the General Court had adopted so many of the English customs and mannerisms that they were almost incapable of identifying with their own people.

The Sakonnets and Pocassets, two of the largest and most powerful of the tribes in the Wampanoag Federation, rendered the Indian cause only lip service until their leaders were caught up in the enthusiasm generated by the younger men when the war broke out close to their territories. Even then, the Sakonnet leaders abandoned Philip at their earliest opportunity, and were instrumental in bringing about his eventual defeat.

The Sakonnet Sachemship included most of the lands on the peninsula on which Little Compton, Rhode Island is now located, and among the tribes in the Wampanoag Federation they were second only to the Pocassets in point of population, and second to none in their martial spirit. Their willingness and ability to fight were vital ingredients in their struggle for survival, for the Narragansetts had tried to take over their lands for many years, and only the valor of the Sakonett warriors prevented them from achieving their goal. That members of these two rival tribes were eventually allied in a common cause against the English has to be attributed to Philip's consummate skill as a diplomat, for it was he who had persuaded them to forget their past differences until New England was forever rid of the hated white men.

The English began to mistrust the Sakonnets as early as 1671, for when Plymouth ordered the members of the Wampanoag Federation to surrender their guns in that year, Tokamona, Sachem of the Sakonnets, refused to do so, and the colony sent a company of soldiers to Sakonnet to force him to comply with their directive.

The soldiers first stopped at a village ruled by Awashonks, a sister of Tokamona, and she, of a much less belligerent nature than her brother, readily accompanied them to Plymouth where she and the warriors with her surrendered all their guns. She also signed a treaty, dated July 24, 1871, in which she acknowledged her submission to the authority of King Charles and in which she promised to send to Plymouth within ten days all the rest of the guns belonging to her people.

When she returned to her village, she ran into a great deal of opposition to the disarmament clause in the treaty, and she was able to convince only 42 of her warriors to surrender their weapons to the English. Most of her people refused, knowing they would be helpless to prevent a Narragansett takeover of their lands if they did, and some of her warriors were so incensed by her capitulation to the English demands that she now lived in constant fear for her life. On August 11, she wrote to Governor Prence to say she had 42 guns which she had tried to send to Plymouth some time earlier. The first English official she contacted refused to accept them, stating that he had no authority to do so. Another official promised to take them, but found they were too heavy for him to carry. All the guns, with the exception of one, were still in her wigwam, waiting for someone to take them to Plymouth. The gun that was missing had been stolen by one of her men during the night, and he had then defected to Mount Hope. She told of the various threats against her life, but assured him she would remain faithful to the terms of the treaty in spite of them.

Governor Prence answered her letter on October 20. He promised that as long as she kept her word, she would have nothing to fear from Plymouth, and he assured her that the colony would always protect her from any danger posed by her enemies. He added that he was sorry to see that her brother and her two sons were among those who had not yet signed the treaty. He did not understand why they refused to acknowledge and submit to the King's authority, but he hoped they would reconsider their attitudes before the English authorities became displeased and sent soldiers to enforce their demands.

When Philip learned of Tokamona's stand against the English, he persuaded the Sakonnet that it would be in the Indians' best interest for him to show at least a semblance of friendship toward the colony, and the two men then travelled to Plymouth where they signed a treaty of submission on November 3. This treaty specified that Tokamona agreed to abide by all the terms of the one Philip had signed on September 29, and that he would order his warriors to surrender their guns to the English as soon as possible. In order to lull Plymouth's suspicions about him, Tokamona sent a number of old, cumbersome weapons to that town, but retained the more modern guns he owned.

Tokamona was killed by the Narragansetts in 1674, and Awashonks succeeded him as leader of the Sakonnets. She was so obviously pro-English that some of her Councilors became disturbed, and tried to change her attitude. When she refused to do so, two of them went to Mount Hope where they pleaded with Philip to send some of his more eloquent emissaries to Sakonnet to win her over, and Philip sent six of his Councilors to attempt this very important diplomatic mission.

BENJAMIN CHURCH'S INFLUENCE ON THE INDIANS

In 1674, Benjamin Church bought a parcel of land on the Sakonnet peninsula where he built a home for his family. He soon won the respect and friendship both of the Sakonnets, whose main village was south of his home, and of the Pocassets, who owned the territory to the north. In the spring of 1675, Governor Prence asked Church to use his friendship with the Sakonnets and the Pocassets to persuade them to remain neutral in the war that now seemed inevitable.

Church first went to Sakonnet where he was astounded to see such a large concentration of warriors. As he soon found out, the reason they were here was that the Pokanoket war messengers had already arrived, and Awashonks had called her Council together to listen to them. Among those present were her husband, Tolony, and two of her sons. The older, Peter, was the chief War Captain of the Sakonnets, while the younger, William, was a brilliant scholar who had attended the Indian Charity School in Cambridge, but who had to abandon his studies because of poor health.

Church quickly realized that he had blundered into a Council of War, but fearing he would be killed if he showed any signs of fear, he strode boldly to the Council Fire where Awashonks was leading her men in a dance. When she was told that Church had come to see her, she sat down, ordered her Councilors about her, and invited the Englishman to sit next to her.

She explained that her Council was in session because Philip had sent six war messengers to persuade her to join him in a war against the English. When she expressed doubts about joining the movement, the messengers told her that Plymouth had already conscripted a huge army that would soon be sent against the Sakonnets, knowing that they could more easily subdue them by a sneak attack than by an open declaration of war.

Church told her there was no truth to this story, for he had just come from Plymouth, and he had seen no preparations for war taking place while he was there. He asked her if she thought he would be stupid enough to risk his life by coming here if he knew that a war might erupt at any moment?

The Squaw-Sachem sat silent for some time, then ordered Philip's messengers to appear before the Council. They came at once, their faces covered with hideous red and black designs, their scalps shaved so that only a single, narrow tuft of hair, much like the comb of a rooster, remained, and carrying powder horns and shot bags on their back to symbolize their position as war messengers.

Without preamble, Awashonks accused them of lying to her, for Church had assured her there were no preparations for war going on at Plymouth. When the Pokanokets realized she had told Church of Philip's plans, they became angry, but were careful to direct their anger at Church rather than at Awashonks. After they had shouted threats at Church for some time, Awashonks commanded them to be quiet. Turning to the Englishman, she told him that the Pokanokets had warned her that if she did not actively espouse Philip's cause, the Great Sachem would send war parties into the area to burn the settlers' homes and kill their cattle and make it appear that the Sakonnets had committed these acts. Then, the English would be sure to declare war on the Sakonnets.

Church walked over to the nearest Pokanoket, hefted the shot bag at his back, and asked him what it contained. The Indian haughtily replied that it held bullets with which he intended to shoot pigeons, intimating that the pigeons were the English colonists. Church turned to Awashonks and told her that Philip could not hope to win a war against the English since there were so many more Englishmen than Indians in New England. He told her she would do well to remain under the protection of the English, and could show her good faith toward them by killing the six Pokanokets right away. This would guarantee that her tribe would still be intact long after those who fought against the English were destroyed.

Although the Pokanokets realized that Church might be able to influence Awashonks, they knew they were in no immediate danger. Since they had been brought to the Council as guests of two of its members, the Sakonnets could not harm them in spite of Awashonks' wishes in the matter. In fact, the Sakonnets were responsible for their safety until they returned to Mount Hope. On the other hand, Church was not an invited guest, but had come to the village voluntarily. Although he was there as an emissary of the Plymouth Governor, it was not in an official capacity, and he therefore did not enjoy the same immunity under Indian law.

One of the Sakonnet Councilors named Little Eyes became so angry at Church's suggestion that he rushed at him with his tomahawk upraised, and the Englishman might have been killed had it not been for the quick action of another Councilor who blocked his way. Little Eyes returned to his seat, remained quiet for a few seconds, then in a calm voice asked Church if he might speak with him in private. The Councilor who had saved Church's life told the Englishman that Little Eyes had already openly allied himself with Philip, and for this reason was not to be trusted. It was obvious that he wanted to be alone with Church so he could kill him.

Church thanked him for his advice, then turned to the Pokanokets. He told them, "You are bloody wretches, and thirst after the blood of your English neighbors who have never injured you and have shown you nothing but kindness. However, if nothing but war will satisfy you, I believe you will find me a sharp thorn in your sides."

He advised Awashonks to send her most trusted Councilors

to Plymouth to ask for protection, warning her again not to join in the rebellion when it began, since the Indians could not possibly win a war against the English.

Convinced by his earnest manner, Awashonks thanked him and asked him to assure the Governor that she was completely loyal to the English. He promised that he would pass on the message and that he would return to Sakonnet as soon as he possibly could.

Fearing that he was in danger of being attacked and killed by some of her men, she sent five of her most trusted men to accompany him to his home.

Church next travelled to Pocasset. As he neared the main village, he met Petanunuit, Weetamoo's husband. Although he was King Philip's brother-in-law, Petanunuit's sympathies were with the English. He told Church that he had just returned from Mount Hope where Philip was then conducting a War Dance. He begged Church to speak to Weetamoo, and convince her of the futility of siding with Philip if the war actually started. Since Church's purpose in coming was to convince Weetamoo of this, he accompanied Petanunuit to his home. When they arrived at Pocasset, the village was deserted except for Weetamoo and some women and children. She told Church that her warriors had all gone to Pokanoket to take part in the War Dance, and she was so confused by the speed with which events were taking place that she was not certain where her best interests lay.

Church spoke to her for some time, explaining, as he had to Awashonks, that it was impossible for the Indians to win a war against the English, and he at last received her promise that she would remain neutral when the war began. He told her he would report her attitude to the English authorities, and he assured her he would return to her as soon as he possibly could. He then continued on to Plymouth where he arrived on June 7.

After reporting to the Governor, he made plans to return to his home, but the war broke out before he left, and he accepted a commission as a captain in the Plymouth company that was sent to Pokanoket to fight against Philip.

THE DECLINE OF THE MASSACHUSETTS FEDERATION

Because their contacts with the outside world were practically non-existent until almost the middle of the 17th century, much less is known about the Nipmuck (Freshwater)

Indians who lived in the interior sections of Massachusetts and Connecticut than of the tribes that lived along the New England coast. Although these inland Indians are generally referred to collectively as being part of the Nipmuck Nation, there is no proof that they ever formed an effective federation of their own, for even when they were at their greatest strength in 1615, most of them were members of the Massachusetts Federation over which Nanepashemet ruled as Great Sachem.

His empire, also at the peak of its power during that same year, extended roughly from Weymouth, Mass. to Portsmouth, N.H. in the east, and from Thompsonville, Connecticut to Northfield, Mass. in the west, embracing a territory of approximately 6,000 square miles which made it, quite possibly, the largest in New England, not only in point of area but in population, as well.

Because of their fortunate geographic location, the Massachusetts were an industrious and peaceful people. To the south of them were the Wampanoags who were forced to direct the major part of their war-making capabilities against their ancient enemies, the Narragansetts. Because of this, they remained more or less at peace with the Massachusetts who were careful not to antagonize the Wampanoags by encroaching on their lands. In the west, the Connecticut River acted as a natural barrier against incursions by the Iroquois of New York, a confederation whose military exploits had extended their sphere of influence in New England to the western banks of that river. The Piscataqua River separated and helped to protect them from attack by the Penobscots who ranged the coast of Maine as far north as the river from which they received their name. The Tarratines, the most vicious and warlike of all the New England tribes, lived to the north of the Penobscots, who were forced to maintain a constant vigil along the banks of the river that separated them. As was the case with the Wampanoags, the Penobscots were kept so busy defending themselves from the Tarratines that they had no desire to cause trouble for the Massachusetts.

In spite of their auspicious circumstances, the Massachusetts were not a decadent people, for many of the early explorers and traders who visited New England during these years were impressed not only by the beauty of the natives but by their industry and their bravery. One of these was Captain John Smith. In 1614, he led two ships to Maine to fish and trade for furs, and when he returned to England, he published a map of New England plus a fairly detailed description of the country and the people living here. He wrote that he saw more than 30 villages on the banks of the Merrimack River, all of whom were members of the Massachusetts Federation. He was particularly impressed with the lands and people in and about Massachusetts Bay, stating, "And then the country of the Massachusetts which is the paradise of all those parts; for here are many Isles all planted with Corn; groves, mulberries, savage gardens, and good harbors ... The sea coast as you pass, shows you all along large corn fields, and great troops of well proportioned people ... We found the people in these parts very kind; but in their fury no less valiant, for, upon a quarrel we had with one of them, he only with three others crossed the harbor to Quonohassit (Cohasset) to certain rocks whereby we must pass, and there let fly their arrows for our shot, till we were out of danger."

The idyllic existence of the Massachusetts ended in 1615, for in that year the Tarratines went to war against the Penobscots, a war they prosecuted with so much vigor and enthusiasm that the Penobscots were defeated within a very short time. Once started on their orgy of murder and destruction, the Tarratines refused to stop, and they carried the war to most of the coastal villages of the Massachusetts and even to some of the Wampanoags.

Such was their lust for blood that the coast of New England was literally strewn with bodies of thousands of their victims before they finally returned to Maine.

The following year, the New England Indians were attacked by a disease that killed thousands more during the three years that elapsed before it finally ran its course. Even while the disease was claiming such a dreadful toll, the Tarratines returned to harass the Massachusetts at frequent intervals, determined to kill those of their leaders who had survived their first raids.

Nanepashemet was unable to raise an army large enough to defend his people from the Tarratines, for just the sound of their name was enough to send even the bravest warriors into a frenzy of fear, and he became so concerned for the safety of his family that he sent them to live with one of the inland tribes. He then abandoned his various homes along the coast to retire to Medford where he built several fortresses. In some respects, these were similar to the European castles of the Middle Ages even to the wide moat that surrounded each one.

The complicated precautions he took to protect himself proved to be useless, for in 1619 the Tarratines finally tracked him down, successfully assaulted the fortress where he was hiding, and killed him.

During the years that Nanepashemet remained in hiding, his empire began to disintegrate, and his death helped to complete the destruction started during his self-imposed exile. His widow, known to history only as Squaw-Sachem of Massachusetts, returned to Medford after the Tarratines left, and tried to gather under her rule all the tribes that were once a part of the Massachusetts Federation. Her efforts were only partially successful, for only a few minor tribes along the North Shore of Massachusetts were willing to accept her as their leader. All the rest had long since formed new alliances. Those tribes living along the banks of the Merrimack River in the northeastern section of Massachusetts were now banded together in a federation known as the Pawtucket over which Passaconaway ruled as Great Sachem, while those along the south shore had chosen Chikataubut, Sachem of Passonagessit, to be their leader. Since the seat of government of this federation was on the shores of Massachusetts Bay, it, too, was known as the Massachusetts. Some of the tribes became tributary to the Wampanoags, while others submitted themselves to the authority of the powerful Narragansetts over which Tasstussuch then ruled as Great Sachem. Squaw-Sachem carried on a series of raids against those of her neighbors who had defected from her federation, but the fact that she, too, was forced to go into hiding whenever the Tarratines appeared made it impossible for her to win any of them back. The makeup of the New England Federations remained fairly static until the Pequots of Connecticut began to reach their greatest strength between 1625 and 1630. During these years, the leaders of this vigorous young tribe sent their war parties as far north along the Connecticut River as Northfield, Mass., and forced most of the Nipmuck tribes living along the banks of this river to become tributary to them. They remained in submission to the Pequots until 1636 when the English colonists declared war on the Pequots and destroyed the power of the federation during the Pequot-Mohican War.

The remnants of this once-great Nation were later gathered together by Uncas, Sachem of the Connecticut Mohicans, and he carried on a long-term feud with Massasoit and Alexander over the right to rule a number of the Nipmuck tribes. Since most of the Nipmucks living in Massachusetts preferred to be allied with Massasoit, several minor clashes occurred between the Wampanoags and the Mohicans. The Massachusetts authorities had no desire to see a war break out between these two federations, both of whom had shown their friendship for the English on a number of occasions, and they stepped in and mediated the dispute, forcing Massasoit and Uncas to abide by their ruling.

THE ENGLISH DESTROY THE PEQUOT FEDERATION

When the Puritans settled in and around Boston in 1630, the Indian population had been drastically reduced. Most of the villages where John Smith had seen "great troops of well proportioned people" only 16 years earlier, were now abandoned, for some of the tribes had been so devastated by the Tarratine raids and the Plague that they no longer existed.

Those of these tribes who survived the two calamities were soon assimilated by other nearby tribes, and although the various Sachems still claimed the lands that were theirs by right of inheritance, they had little or no use for them other than as hunting or fishing grounds. This meant that the Puritans had much less trouble finding lands on which to accommodate their rapidly expanding population than they might have, had the Indians been as plentiful as they were in 1614. In fact, Wonohaquaham, Sachem of the Winnisimmets, gladly allowed the Puritans to settle on what is now Charlestown, for he hoped they would help defend him against the Tarratines, who continued to harass the Massachusetts Indians at least once each year, usually when their crops were ready to be harvested.

In 1633, the few Indians who still lived along the shores of Massachusetts Bay were further reduced by an outbreak of small-pox, and the Puritans were now able to settle almost any part of eastern Massachusetts without the formality of written deeds.

In spite of the drastic reduction in the Indian population, enough of them still remained to challenge the proselityzing zeal of some of the ministers. When the Massachusetts Bay Company was first granted a Royal charter by Charles I, one of the clauses in the charter stated that the colony proposed for New England should be so "religiously and civilly governed as the good life and orderly conversation of the inhabitants might invite the natives to the knowledge of the Christian faith; which, in the Royal intention...was the principal end of the plantation." While the Puritan leaders were still in England, they seemed anxious to begin the task of Christianizing the Indians, but after they settled in Massachusetts, they became so caught up in their own struggle for existence, that they had little or no time to spare for this work. Indeed, many of them soon became convinced that the many differences in their culture and that of the natives made it impractical for the two people to coexist as neighbors.

The influx of new immigrants was so great during the early years that by 1636 more lands were needed to accommodate them, and the Pequot-Mohican War of 1636-1637 was started in an unabashed bid for the rich lands along the banks of the Connecticut River in Massachusetts and Connecticut. Once the Pequots were defeated, the colonists made certain that this once-powerful federation would never again pose a threat to their security by selling a large number of the Pequots into slavery.

John Mason, the leader of the Connecticut troops who mercilessly slaughtered 700 men, women, and children at Mistick Fort, the largest single action of that war, wrote, "Thus was God seen in the Mount, crushing His proud enemies." His was the popular attitude of that time, for many of the New England ministers were convinced that God had sent the Plague among the Indians to make room for His chosen people, the Puritans, and most of them invariably drew analogies in their sermons between the ancient Israelites and the English settlers.

In spite of these prevalent beliefs, there were clergymen in the colony who wanted to begin missionary work among the Indians as soon as it was humanly possible to do so. Some of these men might have been motivated by a desire to please the King and the Anglican Bishops, for these religious leaders were anxious to compile a record of conversions as impressive as those of the Catholic Spaniards and French in the territories they occupied. The Reverend John Eliot, pastor of the Roxbury Church, was not one of these. This saintly man hoped not only to convert the nearby Indians to Christianity, but also to raise their standard of living to the level enjoyed by the settlers. Aware that he would have difficulty in accomplishing this goal unless he could communicate with them in their own language, he purchased a young Montauk prisoner-of-war named Cheekanoe during the Pequot-Mohican War so that he might learn the language from him.

When he discovered the many differences between the Montauk and the Massachusetts dialects, he gave Cheekanoe his freedom, and engaged another Indian to act as his instructor, this one a Massachusetts named Job Nesutan. Nesutan became so devoted to Mr. Eliot that he remained in his employ for more than 35 years. During these years, he served not only as Mr. Eliot's tutor, but also as his chief assistant in the many projects the "Apostle to the Indians" undertook, one of which was the herculean task of translating the Bible into the Indian language.

INDIAN-ENGLISH RELATIONS BECOME STRAINED

The years immediately following the Pequot-Mohican War proved to be an uneasy period in English-Indian relations. The colonists were uncertain how the majority of the tribes would react to the brutal manner in which the Pequot Federation had been destroyed, and they were quick to sense even the most subtle changes in Indian behavior. Frequent reports came to Boston that the Indians were plotting to rebel against the English, and the colonists managed to antagonize the leaders of some of the nearby tribes by the insensitive manner in which they investigated these rumors, a fact that made Eliot's work more difficult than it might have been.

In 1642, the Connecticut authorities received reports from three different Indians warning them that the New England Indians were plotting to unite in a war against the colonists. Properly alarmed, they quickly sent word to Boston, and on the basis of these vague, unconfirmed rumors, Massachusetts sent an armed force of 40 men to arrest Cutchamakin, Sachem of the Braintree Indians. The soldiers first seized all the guns owned by his people, then brought him to Boston for questioning. After he proved that he knew nothing of a plot, he was set free, and allowed to return to Braintree. He had no sooner arrived at his village than some soldiers appeared, bringing with them the guns they had taken earlier, to request his aid as a guide and interpreter at other Indian villages.

He agreed to do so, and accompanied the soldiers to Ipswich where they disarmed the Agawam Indians, then travelled inland to Merrimack where Passaconaway was then living on an island in the middle of the Merrimack River. The stream was so swollen and turbulent from recent heavy rains that the soldiers were afraid to venture onto it in the flimsy Indian canoes available to them. As they milled about uncertainly, Cutchamakin told them that Wannalancet,

Passaconaway's son, lived nearby in a village much more easily accessible then his father's island retreat. The soldiers immediately marched to this village, and seized Wannalancet, his wife, and his infant son.

One of the leaders argued that they had no authority to take women and children as hostages, and after a lengthy discussion, the young woman and her child were released. Unable to understand why she had been detained or set free, the terror-stricken girl fled into the forest as soon as she was released, and she remained there for ten days before hunger and concern for the well being of her child forced her to return to her village.

In the meanwhile, the soldiers began the long journey back to Boston with their prisoner. Because Cutchamakin had warned them that Wannalancet was as skilled in the arts of magic as his father, they fastened his hands securely behind his back, and led him by a noose tied around his neck. As a further precaution, they assigned a squad of men to keep him under constant surveillance, but in spite of these security measures, he slipped his bonds, and escaped into the woods in broad daylight, unharmed by the hail of bullets fired at him as he fled.

The news that the soldiers brought back to Boston alarmed the Puritans, and properly so, for Passaconaway's reputation as a warrior was such that even the Mohawks refused to be drawn into a war against him. The authorities feared that the proud Sachem might seek revenge for his son's ill-treatment by attacking one or more of the frontier settlements, and they sent Cutchamakin to him to explain that the English wished to remain on friendly terms with his people.

When Cutchamakin arrived at Merrimack, he told Passaconaway that the soldiers had captured Wannalancet only so they could question him, and he assured him they would have released him unharmed once they were convinced he was not involved in a plot against them. His escape only served to arouse the suspicions of the authorites, for they now felt that the Pawtuckets were concealing information that was vital to the safety of the colonists. Because of this, they refused to consider the matter closed, and demanded that Passaconaway or a high-ranking member of his Council come to Boston for questioning. If he refused to cooperate with them, they would send a large army to destroy the Pawtuckets.

Cutchamakin pleaded with the Pawtucket leader to avoid a needless confrontation, for he could prove his good intentions by surrendering his guns, and accompanying him to Boston. Although Passaconaway did not want to provoke the English into a war, he stubbornly told Cutchamakin that he would not talk to the English until his son, daughter-in-law, and grandson were returned unharmed to their village.

A crisis was happily averted when Wannalancet went to Boston without his father's knowledge. He first surrendered his guns, then submitted to an intensive interrogation. When he proved to their complete satisfaction that he knew nothing of a planned rebellion, they gave back his weapons, and allowed him to return to his village.

The Reverend John Eliot visited the Pawtuckets some time after this, and although Passaconaway received him very cooly at first, his attitude changed as time went on. The Great Sachem was so impressed by Eliot that the two soon became fast friends, and tradition has it that Passaconaway agreed to accept the Christian religion as his own several years before he died.

THE PRAYING INDIAN VILLAGES

In 1644, even more rumors were heard of Indian uprisings. Hoping to forestall a concerted rebellion, Massachusetts initiated a series of treaties with the leaders of many of the Nipmuck and Massachusetts tribes. Among the first of those who agreed to submit to the authority of the English King was Cutchamakin, and he was soon after followed by Masconomo, Sachem of Agawam, Squaw-Sachem of Massachusetts, and Josias, Sachem of Passonagessit. Other Sachems soon followed their lead, and the serious troubles with the Indians appeared to be ended. The treaties stipulated that the Sachems would accept the English God as their own, would observe the commandments, and would allow their children to read and study the Bible. Strangely enough, it was the English who found it difficult to carry out their part of the treaty, even though the authorities directed the County Courts to prepare for the task of civilizing the Indians and instructing them in the knowledge and proper worship of God.

During this period, Eliot became so proficient in the Massachusetts dialect that he began to hold lengthy conversations with his instructor, a fact that convinced him that he was now ready to start preaching to the Indians in their own language. Waban, a member of the Nonantum (Newton) Indians, invited him to give his first sermon at his lodge, and Eliot did so on October 28, 1646. The Indians reacted so favorably, impressed by the pains he had taken to learn their language, that he preached four more times before the year was out, each time to progressively larger audiences. His success encouraged the General Court to pass an act for the Propagation of the Gospel among the Indians that same year, an act that urged the elders of the various churches in the colony to take an active role in implementing Eliot's work.

The English clergy was pleased at the news of his success, and to stimulate him and the other New England evangelists on to greater efforts, they persuaded Oliver Cromwell to push an ordinance through the Parliament to help them financially. That body formed "The Corporation for the Promoting and Propagating the Gospel of Jesus Christ in New England", an organization that managed to raise almost 12,000 pounds within the next ten years. Approximately 5,000 pounds of this was sent to the Commissioners of the United Colonies who were authorized to distribute it as they saw fit, and much of this sum was eventually given to John Eliot. Although Eliot often complained that many of his converts reverted to their own religion once he left their village to travel to another, his efforts were deemed so successful in England that Charles II allowed the corporation to continue when he was restored to the throne in 1661.

A number of Eliot's Indian converts became imbued with his missionary zeal, and travelled throughout New England to prepare the way for him. Unfortunately, some of these men attacked their work so enthusiastically that many of the Sachems reacted adversely. Uncas, Canonicus, Ninigret, and Massasoit were among those who were unalterably opposed to the introduction of this alien religion among their people, for they were convinced that no one God, regardless of how powerful he might be, could be as effective as their own 37 gods.

The Pow-wows were even more strongly opposed to Christianity than the Great Sachems, for their wealth and power came from the gifts they exacted from those for whom they acted as intermediaries with Hobbamocko, who can best be described as the Indian equivalent of the Christian devil.

Kichtan, the Supreme Deity, and Hobbamocko were the two most important gods in southeastern New England Indian theology. The Indians believed that all the gods were fashioned by Kichtan, who also predestined the fate of all his people. Although he was a gentle and loving god, he would not alter anyone's fate regardless of how many prayers or sacrifices were offered up to him. Because of this, the Indians largely ignored him, and directed their pleas for help to Hobbamocko. It was no easy matter to gain his favorable attention, however, for only the Pow-wows were allowed to communicate with him, and they would do so only if suitably rich gifts were given them. Since these were to be shared equally with Hobbamocko, the Indians willingly gave whatever was demanded even if Hobbamocko did not or was unable to help them.

The Pow-wows used various means to hinder the spread of the Gospel, and to reclaim those who had succumbed to the blandishments of the missionaries. One Pow-wow did so by having Hobbamocko's spectre appear before a number of Massachusetts apostates and threaten to punish them if they did not return to their own religion. They were told that they could not go to the meetinghouse where they were taught to read and write, nor could they attend any more Christian services. His visit was so effective that none of these people was ever again tempted to deviate from the Indian religion. A Rhode Island Pow-wow also used Hobbamocko's apparition to warn a group of Christian Indians that they could no longer practice this alien religion. When he later learned they had disobeyed him, he spirited them away during a violent storm, and they were never again heard from.

Eliot's work suffered so much from these and similar tactics that some of his helpers attempted to offset their effects by employing methods that were equally reprehensible. When the Narragansett leaders learned of them, they turned to Roger Williams for help. Knowing that he was going to visit England, they begged him to intercede with the English King on their behalf. Williams later wrote to Governor Winthrop, "At my last departure for England, I was importuned by the Narragansetts, and especially Nenecaut (Ninigret)', to present their petitions to the high Sachems of England, that they might not be forced from their religion; and for not changing their religion, be invaded by war. For they said they were daily visited by threatening Indians from about the Massachusetts; that if they would not pray, they would be destroyed by war ...

Are not all the English of this land, (generally), a persecuted people from their native soil? and hath not the God of peace and Father of mercies made the natives more friendly in this than our native country men in our own land to us? have they not entered leagues of love, and our families grown up in peace among them? Upon which I humbly ask how it can suit with Christian ingenuity, to take hold of some seeming occasion for their destruction.''

Agreeing that these tactics were distasteful, the Massachusetts General Court passed a law in 1646 prohibiting the use of threats or force to convert Indians to the Christian religion, but they tempered this liberal legislation by also ruling that all Indians living within the jurisdiction of the colony were forbidden to worship their false gods, and that the Pow-wows, who they considered to be devil worshippers, could no longer conduct their native religious services.

As relations between the Massachusetts colonists and the Indians became less strained, Eliot began to plan several projects for the good of his converts. Second in importance only to translating the Bible into the Indian language was his plan for an Indian village that would be patterned after the English settlements, and which would be governed almost completely by the Indians living in it. Here they would not only be given the opportunity to learn to read and write, but would be taught all the crafts needed to make their community as nearly self-sustaining as possible. In 1651, the General Court granted him a charter to build such a town on 6,000 acres of land lying on both sides of the Charles River in Natick. The Indians first built an arched foot-bridge, 80 feet long and eight feet high, across the river, and they constructed it so sturdily that it was still usable long after others, built at approximately the same time by English workers, had been swept away by unexpected freshets or other climatic phenomena.

They next built a palisaded fort and a meetinghouse. The first floor of the meetinghouse was used as a schoolroom and as a place of worship, while the second floor, except for a corner that was set aside as an apartment for Mr. Eliot, was used as a communal warehouse for storing furs and other valuables.

The town consisted of three long streets running parallel to each other—two of them on the north side of the river, the other on the south side. Each family was given a lot of land on which to build a home, and after the village was fenced in, the Indians began to build their houses. Some copied those of their English neighbors, but the majority built wigwams since these could be erected much more quickly and economically, and could be kept warm in the winter much more easily than the English-type dwellings. Once their homes were completed, the Indians planted a number of fruit trees, and then broke ground in the common lands for their cornfields.

At Eliot's suggestion, the Indians patterned their government after that of the early Israelites, who had rulers of tens, fifties, hundreds, etc. After they had chosen their leaders, they appointed a teacher for their school, and Eliot's dream was at last a reality. The Natick experiment was so successful, that Eliot was encouraged to start others in different parts of the colony, and those who lived in these Christian Indian villages were so content in their new surroundings that they willingly agreed to accept English laws as well as the English religion.

By 1675, there were seven Praying Indian villages throughout Massachusetts. These were Natick, Nashoba (Littleton), Wamesit, Hassanamessit (Grafton), Okommakamesit (Marlborough), Hakunkokoag (Hopkinton), and Punkapoag (Canton), and were known as the "Old Praying Villages." In addition to these, nine others, known as the "New Praying Villages," were at Manchaug (Sutton), Chaubunagungamaug (Webster), Maanexit (Woodstock, Conn.), Waentug (Uxbridge), Quantisset (Thompson, Conn.), Wabaquasset (Woodstock, Conn), Quaboag (Brookfield), Pakachoog (Worcester), and Nashaway (Lancaster). Daniel Gookin, a neighbor and close friend of Eliot, was appointed Commissioner of Indian Affairs, and he proved to be as sincere a friend to the Indians as Eliot.

There were also several Praying Indian villages in Plymouth Colony. Most of these were so small that they should more properly be classified as hamlets, and those living in them usually held their church services in conjunction with those of other small communities. For example, those living at Meeshawn (Truro) combined with those living at Punonokanit (South Wellflett); those at Potanumquot (South Orleans) with those at Nawsett (Eastham); those at Sawkatuckett (Dennis), Nobsquassit (North Dennis), and Matakees (Yarmouth) with those at Weequakutt (Barnstable); those at Satuit (Mashpee), Pawpoesit (Mashpee), Mashpee (Mashpee), Coatuit

(Osterville) with those at Waquoit (Falmouth), those at Codtanmut (Mashpee) and Ashimuit (Falmouth) with those at Weesquobs (Mashpee); those at Pispogutt and Wawayontat (both Wareham) with those at Sokones (Falmouth); and those at Ketchiquut or Titicut (Middleboro) with those at Assawamsoo (Lakeville). The village of Manamoyick (Chatham) was the only one with a congregation large enough to support its own church.

There were also Indian Praying villages on Martha's Vineyard and Nantucket. These Indians were converted through the efforts of Thomas Mayhew and his son, Reverend Thomas Mayhew, Jr. The senior Mayhew purchased Martha's Vineyard, Nantucket, and the Elizabeth Islands in 1641, and his son went there the following year to prepare a settlement for his father and his family. The younger Mayhew, of a sincerely compassionate nature, was so moved by the abject poverty of the Indians on these islands that he quickly learned their language so he would be better able to help them.

He gained his first convert to Christianity in 1643, three years before Eliot began preaching to the Massachusetts and the Nipmucks, and in 1652, he opened a school where Indian children were taught to read and write. When he was lost at sea in 1657, his father continued on with his work, and he was so successful that just before the start of the King Philip War there were two churches on Martha's Vineyard and two more on Nantucket serving the Indians of Chappaquiddick Island, Nashamoiess (Edgartown), Sangekontakit (Edgartown), Toikiming (West Tisbury), Nashakemmiuk (Chilmark), Talhanio (Chilmark), Oggawame (Siasconnett), and Wammasquid (near Miacomet Pond). Such was Mayhew's influence on the Indians of these parishes that they refused to join the patriot Indian effort during the King Philip War, and a large number served in the English army.

THE MASSACHUSETTS—MOHAWK WAR

Of the Indians living in Massachusetts at the start of the war, the Nipmucks and the Massachusetts were among the few who had had any extensive military experience within the past generation, for they had been at war with the Iroquois of New York from 1663 to 1669. This war broke out when the Mohawks, one of the most vigorous and warlike of the five tribes that then comprised the Iroquois Federation, attacked several of the Connecticut River tribes, then demanded tribute in exchange for peace, a practice that had extended their power and influence from Canada to Virginia and as far west as the Mississippi River.

Josias Chikataubut, a great grandson of the original Chikataubut, refused to be intimidated, and encouraged the Nipmucks to fight back. Several minor clashes took place, and although the Mohawks were usually victorious, the Nipmucks became braver when they saw that the Mohawks attacked them at less frequent intervals. Hoping to oust them forever from Massachusetts, Chikataubut raised an army of almost 700 men in 1669, and led them to Mohawk Country near Albany, New York. That he undertook this campaign at all is a tribute not only to his courage, but also to his optimism, for although he was the army's supreme commander, the leaders of the various units of which it was comprised, obeyed his orders only when it suited them. Carried away by his own optimism, however, Chikataubut refused to recognize the danger these undisciplined men posed to a smoothly coordinated and efficient war effort, and made very little effort to correct the situation.

Worse, he made several blunders in planning the campaign, the most serious of which can be attributed to the fact that he knew so little of logistics, for he failed to provide wagons to carry the supplies needed by an army of this size, and this forced the men to carry so much weight that they had to stop at frequent intervals to rest. Many of the older men were unable to withstand the rigors of the march. Some left the main column to rest for several days at a time, hoping to overtake the others before they arrived in Mohawk Country, while others deserted, and returned to their homes.

Since food was in short supply, it was common for whole units to leave the main force for days at a time so the men could fish, hunt, or forage in the woods and swamps for food.

Some of the men could not resist the temptation of stopping at every Indian village close to their line of march to show their friends the huge expedition, the first of its kind to be assembled in New England in many years. They remained at each of these villages for several days, gorging themselves with the food supplied by their hosts, and boasting of the many brave deeds they would perform when they met the enemy.

It took so long for this unlikely task force to arrive at its destination that the Mohawks knew of the planned invasion long before it took place. This gave them ample time to strengthen their already almost-impregnable fortresses, and when the allied army arrived at the Mohawk fort, the enemy was ready for them. They had sent their women and children to another village, filled the fort with their best warriors, and stocked up with enough food and ammunition to carry them through a prolonged seige. The Massachusetts, their supplies at dangerously low levels, wasted no time when they arrived, and mounted several assaults on the fort. They accomplished little or nothing by doing so except to use up ammunition they could ill afford to spare.

Within a few days, Chikataubut realized the expedition was failure. There was very little ammunition left, and most of the men were so ill that he knew many of them would die if he did not abandon the seige at once. He ordered his leaders to move out, and as the men were assembling their gear, the Mohawks erupted from the fort, and attacked them. Chikataubut managed to rally his men about him, and fought back so fiercely that the Mohawks were forced to retreat, leaving a large number of their dead and wounded behind.

After the battle was ended, the Massachusetts salvaged what supplies they could, and began the long march home. The Mohawks sent a large war party to set up an ambush along the trail through which the Massachusetts would have to pass, at a point approximately 30 miles from the Mohawk Fort. When the exhausted and dispirited men blundered into the trap, the Mohawks opened fire, killing 30 of them with the first volley. The Massachusetts might have been annihilated but for the bravery and quick thinking of their leader. When the first shots rang out, Chikataubut led a band of warriors into the swamps where the Mohawks were hiding, and after a fierce hand-to-hand fight that raged for several hours, the Mohawks were again forced to retreat. They had underestimated the fighting ability of the Massachusetts, and were not prepared to cope with Chikataubut's ferocious counterattack. When their War Captains saw that the battle was lost, they wisely ordered their troops to withdraw, unwilling to sacrifice any more lives unnecessarily.

Although this was a decisive victory for the Massachusetts Indians, it was a costly one, for their losses were almost as great as those of the Mohawks. Worse, some of their best men, including the valiant Chikataubut, were among those killed.

The Massachusetts were fortunate in that the Mohawks had met with reverses in so many other areas that they had no desire to continue the war, and in 1671 they asked their English and Dutch friends in Albany to mediate a peace treaty between them and the Massachusetts, a treaty that was formally signed by both sides that same year.

NIPMUCK CONTRIBUTIONS TO THE PATRIOT CAUSE

The Massachusetts authorities were aware of the unrest among the Nipmuck Indians long before Sassamon's three alleged assassins were executed. Waban, who was now an old man and principal leader of the Christian Indian village at Natick, had twice warned Daniel Gookin that Philip's young braves, eager to avenge the wrongs committed against their people by the English, planned to begin hostilities as soon as the trees in the forests had enough foliage to provide a cover for their activities. He also warned that a number of tribes, among them some Nipmucks, had already pledged their support to the planned uprising. When Gookin relayed this news to the authorities the second time, they reacted by sending messengers to the leaders of the Indian villages of Pakachoog, Maanexit, Wabaquasset, Quantisset, Chabonokongkomen, Manchaug, and Hassanamessit in early June to get assurances of their loyalty. In each instance, the leaders were so sincere in their protestations of friendship and so eager to sign new treaties with the English that the colonial authorities were lulled into a false sense of security, convinced that any uprising that might occur would be on a strictly local level.

They failed to take into account the temper of the younger braves throughout New England, even those living in the Praying Indian villages. These young men, their imaginations fired by the stories of ancient deeds of bravery told by the tribal elders, wanted nothing more than to test themselves in battle against the English. Once hostilities began, their enthusiasm for the Great Fight was so infectious that even the older men became imbued with the same spirit, and the Pokanoket war messengers were greeted enthusiastically wherever they travelled throughout New England. By the end of June, only days after the incidents at Swansea, many of the inland tribes were already committed to the war effort, and were planning raids against the English.

Four of the men most dedicated to the Indian cause were Muttawmp, a leader of the Quaboags; Matoonas, the constable of Pakachoog; Monoco (One-eyed John), and

Shoshanim (Sagamore Sam), both leaders of the Nashaways. On July 14, the three last-named men led a raid against Mendon, the first settlement in the Massachusetts Bay Colony to be attacked. They killed six men who were working in their fields, destroyed a number of fields of corn, burned several buildings, then returned to their village near Mount Wachusett.

Matoonas, who was in charge of the raiding party, bore a grudge of several years' standing against the English. Four years earlier, his son was accused of murdering an English settler, and although it was generally known that another man had committed the crime, the authorities made no effort to find him. The young man was tried, found guilty, and hanged. His head was then placed on a pole, and kept on display as a warning to other Indians. Although Matoonas bitterly resented this gross miscarriage of justice, he did not allow his feelings to be known, but stayed on as constable at Pakachoog until the war broke out, when he was one of the first of the Praying Indians to join Philip.

COLONIAL SOLDIERS ARE MASSACRED AT BROOKFIELD

Shortly before the attack at Mendon, Governor Leverett and his Council sent Ephraim Curtis, a young professional hunter who lived in Worcester, to negotiate a meeting between the colonial and Nipmuck leaders. Three Natick Indians were selected to accompany him, and the four men first went to Brookfield where they rested for awhile before continuing on to Quaboag. When they arrived, they found the village deserted, and they pressed on for several more days until they arrived at a small fortified village which the Indians had only recently built. Striding boldly to the center of the village, they saw that more than 200 Indians were assembled. A group of younger braves quickly surrounded them, then pushed and shoved to provoke them into a fight. The messengers refused to be drawn into a confrontation of this sort, and begged to be taken to their leaders. At first, the young warriors refused to let them leave, but after the Naticks had pleaded with them for some time, they at last relented, and escorted the messengers to the Council Fires where Muttawmp was seated with his Councilors.

Throughout most of this first meeting, Muttawmp was almost as discourteous toward the messengers as his warriors, for this was July 14, the day that Mendon was scheduled to be attacked. Although he did not know if the raid was successful or not, he already considered himself at war with the English, convinced that the time for negotiations with them had long since passed.

One of his Councilors told him that it would help the Indian cause if he pretended to be friendly, so he turned to Curtis and told him he would meet with the English negotiators at any time or place they chose. Curtis sped back to Boston to report the success of his mission, and he was then instructed to return to Muttawmp to tell him that the Governor wanted the Indian leaders to meet at Boston as soon as possible.

Although Muttawmp had no intention of honoring this demand, he told Curtis he would follow him to Boston within a week. When Curtis returned to Boston with this information, the authorities unaccountably changed their original plans. Thy now decided to send Captain Edward Hutchinson to negotiate directly with the Indians. Hutchinson owned a large farm in Nipmuck Country where he regularly employed a number of Indians. As he was familiar with so many of them, the authorities were certain that he could negotiate with them in a much more relaxed and friendly atmosphere in their own country than would be possible in Boston where they would be among strangers. Too, most Bostonians were suspicious of all Indians, even those who had proved their friendship to the English, so the authorities decided to keep them away from Boston to minimize the possibility of any incidents that might antagonize potential allies.

Since it would not be wise for Hutchinson to go into hostile country without an escort, the authorities sent Captain Thomas Wheeler with a troop of 30 horses to accompany him. The negotiators arrived at the New Norwich fortress on July 31, only to find it deserted. Since they had no idea where the Indians might be, they went to Brookfield where they learned that the Indians were now living in a fortress they had only recently built in the middle of a swamp about ten miles away.

So that the Indians would not be frightened by a show of military strength, Hutchinson sent Curtis and three Naticks, under a flag of truce, to arrange for a meeting with their leaders. When the men arrived at the village they found the Indians in a decidedly hostile mood. The younger braves again shoved and pushed Curtis to provoke him into a quarrel, but he controlled his temper, and told them that since he had arrived under a flag of truce, they should treat him with all the courtesy ordinarily accorded an ambassador from another country. Impressed by this logic, the warriors escorted him to the Council Fires where Muttawmp welcomed him courteously. When Curtis told him that Hutchinson, who had been chosen to represent the English in negotiating with the Indians, was in Brookfield, Muttawmp agreed to meet him at eight o'clock the following morning on a plain near the northern end of Wickabaug Pond in West Brookfield. This was agreeable to Curtis, and he returned to Brookfield with the news.

The entire company marched to the appointed place the following morning, but again could find no trace of the Indians. The Naticks, who were serving as guides for the company, pleaded with Hutchinson to return to Brookfield at once. They told him that there were signs that a number of Indians had just recently been in the vicinity, and they suspected these Indians had laid a trap somewhere ahead. The Brookfield men who were now with the party scoffed at the idea of danger, claiming that the Quaboags were good Christians who were incapable of treachery. They argued so earnestly that Hutchinson agreed to go on, but only as far as their new fortress.

When the soldiers arrived at the edge of the swamp, they found the path leading into it so narrow that they could pass through only in a single file. The path was bounded on the left by a thick swamp, and on the right by a steep, rock-filled hill. This was such an obviously dangerous place that Hutchinson and Wheeler debated the advisability of continuing on. Again, the Naticks urged them to abandon the mission, arguing that this kind of terrain readily lent itself to ambush, but the Brookfield men argued just as vehemently that they were in no danger. Although Hutchinson and Wheeler knew the risks involved, they also felt that their mission would in all probability be doomed to failure if they postponed their meeting with Muttawmp to a later date, and they agreed to continue on a few miles more before returning to Brookfield.

They had advanced about 400 yards into the swamp when they were attacked by a large force of Indians who suddenly rose from the tall grasses before them. Eight men were killed by the first volley, and five others were wounded. When the surviving troopers wheeled about to retreat, they found their way blocked by another band of Indians who poured round after round of shot at them. Muttawmp had laid his trap well, for the English were completely surrounded and in such a state of panic that some time elapsed before they returned the fire. Captain Hutchinson was wounded by the first volley, and although he lingered on for 17 days after the ambush, he eventually died of his wounds. Captain Wheeler also received a serious wound, and his horse was killed during the first few minutes. As he lay helplessly on the ground, his son, also wounded, dismounted, helped his father onto his horse, then mounted another whose rider had been killed. As the soldiers continued to mill about, bewildered by the unexpected attack and by the contradictory orders shouted at them, one of the Naticks took command of the company. Urging the men to follow him, he spurred his horse up the steep hill, then found a little-used trail leading back to Brookfield over which he led the men to safety, well ahead of the pursuing Nipmucks who raced after them on foot.

At the village, the soldiers selected one of the largest houses in which to make their stand. Captain Wheeler had now recovered from the shock of his wounds, and he again assumed command of his men. He ordered some of the men to fortify the house against the expected attack, and sent others through the village to alert the people to their danger. The frightened settlers abandoned their own homes to join the soldiers, none of them thinking to bring extra food, clothing, guns or ammunition, articles that would be vitally necessary if the expected seige lasted any length of time.

When they were crowded into the garrison, Wheeler ordered two men to ride to Marlborough for reinforcements. When the two stepped outside, they saw that the Indians were already at the village, and returned inside to report this fact to Captain Wheeler.

Muttawmp's men were indeed busily at work. Some were rifling the deserted houses, while others were driving the livestock into the woods. Once they had stripped the houses of all the valuables that caught their fancy, they set them afire, then concentrated their attention on the garrison. Muttawmp led his men in three attacks, each of which was driven back.

A number of the Indians were wounded in these attacks, but the English, well-protected as they were, suffered no casualties until late in the day when two of the settlers foolishly stepped out of the house and were instantly killed, the only losses the English sustained during the first day of the seige.

Shortly after midnight, Muttawmp met with his War Captains to discuss strategy. They agreed that it was foolhardy to risk the lives of their men by exposing them to the musket fire of the English at close range, but that it was necessary to force the soldiers out of the house. This had to be done at once, for help was certain to arrive long before they could starve them into submission. One of the Councilors suggested they set the garrison afire, and Muttawmp ordered his best marksmen to shoot flaming arrows at the house. Although some of the arrows became embedded in the roof and the walls, they caused no damage, for the soldiers raced outside and extinguished the flames.

Just before daybreak, Muttawmp ordered his bowmen to stop, then put some of the men to work filling an abandoned farm wagon with highly combustible materials. This was then set afire, and pushed against the garrison. Again, he was thwarted in his plan, this time by the elements, for a sudden heavy shower extinguished the flames before they could ignite the house.

While the Indians focused their attention on the fire wagon, Ephraim Curtis slipped out of the garrison, crawled to the edge of the woods, then ran throughout the rest of the night and part of the morning until he reached Marlborough, a distance of more than 20 miles, where he gasped out his story. His valiant gesture was a wasted one, however, for news of the attack had already been reported by a group of settlers travelling to Connecticut. They heard the sounds of the battle as they passed close to Brookfield where they had intended to spend the night, and they immediately raced to Marlborough with the news. A messenger was dispatched to Major Simon Willard, whose company was then camped near Lancaster, and he and his company were already on their way to Brookfield when Curtis arrived.

Willard and his men reached Brookfield late in the afternoon of August 4, and engaged the Indians in a fierce battle that raged well into the night, but the two forces were so evenly matched that neither was able to gain a permanent advantage over the other.

Since Muttawmp had already accomplished most of his objectives, he refused to risk the loss of more of his men just to gain a meaningless victory, so he retired to one of his fortresses near Hatfield. Before he left, however, he set fire to all the buildings in the town that still remained standing.

The jubilant Indians were no sooner in their fort at Hatfield than they received word that King Philip, accompanied by a retinue of 40 warriors and a number of women and children, would soon appear. When he did arrive, he was told the details of the Brookfield attack, news that pleased him so much that he gave each of the leaders a peck of unstrung wampum, then joined the warriors in a series of shouts, one for each of the English that had been killed in the battle.

ENGLISH INGRATITUDE TOWARD THE NATICKS

The three Naticks whose bravery and quick thinking saved the English troopers from annihilation were George Memecho and two brothers, Sampson and Joseph Robin, none of whom was credited in the dispatches sent to Boston. In fact, they were treated so harshly by the very troopers whose lives they had saved that they later ran off and joined Philip's forces, well aware that the soldiers would find an excuse to kill them if they remained. They did not last long as freedom fighters, however, for Sampson was killed by a group of Christian Indians during the early part of the winter, while Joseph was captured by the English a short time later. He was sent to Boston where he was sold to a West Indian slave trader. Memecho remained with the patriot Indian forces until late spring, when he was at last convinced that the Indian cause was a hopeless one and returned to the English. He told them he had been captured by the Nipmucks shortly after Brookfield, and they had spared his life only because he promised to join them in the war against the colonists. The English believed his story, and also agreed to spare his life in exchange for detailed information about the Indians who were active in Philip's army. After the war, Memecho returned to Natick where he again became a respected member of the community until his death some years later.

THE NEW ENGLAND CONFEDERATION

During the Pequot-Mohican War of 1636-1637, the New England Colonies became aware of how vitally important military preparedness and a union of their forces were to their security and even their existence. It was while this war was still being fought that the organization that became known as the United Colonies of New England was first proposed, although the formal articles of confederation were not signed by the representatives of the four member colonies—

Massachusetts, Plymouth, Connecticut, and New Haven—
until May 29, 1643.

That Providence Plantation (Rhode Island) and Gorgeanna
(York, Maine) were not considered for inclusion is not too
difficult to understand.   Roger Williams, the founder of
Providence Plantation, was expelled from Massachusetts for
advocating religious beliefs that were obnoxious to the
Puritan theocrats, and he compounded this folly by insisting
that the English King had no more right to grant charters that
allowed Englishmen to settle on Indian lands than the
Sachems had to grant charters that permitted Indians to
claim title to any part of England. He further antagonized the
Puritans by granting complete freedom of worship to Jews,
Catholics, and members of other Protestant sects who settled
in Providence.

Georgeanna was excluded for equally important reasons.
Its minister was one who had only a short time before been ex-
communicated by the New England Church and banished
from Massachusetts, while its mayor was only   a common
tailor.   In addition to this, Sir Ferdinando Gorges, the
founder of the colony, was a member of the Anglican Church,
and suspected of having Roman Catholic sympathies.

The preamble to the articles of confederation reads:
"Whereas we all came into these parts of America with one
and the same end, namely, to advance the Kingdom of our
Lord Jesus Christ, and to enjoy the liberties of the gospel in
purity with peace; and whereas by our settling, by the wise
providence of God, we are further dispersed upon the
seacoasts and rivers than was first intended, so that we
cannot, according to our desire with convenience communicate with people of several nations and strange
languages, which hereafter may prove injurious to us or our
posterity; and for as much as the natives have formerly
committed sundry insolences and outrages against several
plantations of the English, and have of late combined
themselves against us, and seeing by reason of the sad
distractions in England (which they have heard of), and by
which they know we are hindered both from the humble way
of seeking advice, and reaping those comfortable fruits of
protection, which at other times we might well expect; we
therefore conceive it our bounden duty, without delay, to
enter into a present consociation amongst ourselves for
mutual help and strength in all future concernment, that, as

in nation and religion, so in other respects, we be and continue one, according to the tenor and true meaning of the ensuing articles..."

Under the terms of the pact, each of the colonies retained its own identity, and continued to exercise jurisdiction over all the settlements that were then or would ever be within its limits. Two commissioners from each colony were to meet with those of the other three at least once each year on the first Thursday in September. They were responsible for keeping an accurate, up-dated tally of all the able-bodied men between the ages of 16 and 60 capable of bearing arms, and were to designate the number each colony was to provide in an emergency.

The men chosen as Commissioners had to be of impeccable character, and members in good standing of the New England Church. Among their other duties, they were authorized to hear, examine, weigh, and determine all affairs of war or peace, pass judgment on those applicants who wished to join the confederation, render military or financial aid when and where needed, conscript the men needed in time of war, and oversee the equitable distribution of the spoils of war.

The colonies had to have trained citizen soldiers who could be ready to take the field at a moment's notice. This attitude of self-sufficiency was not an outgrowth of the United Colonies, but had its beginning many years before. The Pilgrims brought Captain Myles Standish with them in 1620 as commander of all military affairs, and when the Puritans settled the Massachusetts Bay Colony in 1630, they brought two professional soldiers with them, also. Their duties included protecting the civilian population from Indian attack, and their merchant shipping from harassment. During the first years, the two men set up nightly patrols in each settlement, then conducted weekly training drills. These were so effective, that a regular militia was organized in 1636 consisting of one regiment from each of the three counties then comprising the colony--Suffolk, Middlesex, and Essex--and 200 of the best of these men were sent to fight against the Pequots in Connecticut the following year. In 1638, a charter was granted to the train band now known as the Ancient and Honorable Artillery Company, the oldest military organization in continuous operation in North America. Many other companies were formed in the years that followed, most of which mustered on Boston Common each year where they entertained the huge crowds gathered to see them run through their intricate maneuvers.

In 1673, Massachusetts ordered 500 flintlock muskets from England, the first major innovation in weaponry attempted by the colony since 1636. These were much more serviceable than the matchlock muskets they replaced, for the matchlocks were so long and cumbersome that it was necessary for each soldier to carry a tripod or "rest" on which to position the barrel when he fired it. In addition to the heavy iron rest, each soldier carried a bulky knapsack, a leather bandoleer that held 12 or more round boxes, each of which held a single charge of powder, and six feet of fuse to ignite the powder. The matchlocks were not only unwieldy, but required a fairly long time to recharge after each shot.

By 1675, there were 73 well-organized and strongly-disciplined companies in Massachusetts, some comprised of foot soldiers and some of troopers. The foot companies consisted of 70 privates in addition to officers, noncommissioned officers, a drummer, and a company clerk, for a total of well over 90 men, while the cavalry units had 50 privates and a total complement of 70. In time of war, however, the rosters could be and usually were increased by as much as 25 percent.

Until long pikes proved to be of no use in the forests where most of the fighting took place, each foot company had a complement of 15 pikemen. When these were eliminated, the soldiers were given long knives that could be attached to their musket barrels. These were much more effective in close combat than had been anticipated, for the Indians could be held off at a distance great enough so they could not use their knives or tomahawks, and long before the war was ended, the knives were replaced by French bayonnets which the colony imported in great quantities.

THE COLONISTS EXPAND THEIR ARMED FORCES

Only after news of the Brookfield attack reached Boston were the authorities convinced they now had to contend with a general uprising. The Commissioners of the United Colonies, meeting at Boston for the first time since the outbreak of hostilities, now assumed their duties as leaders of the allied war effort, and they immediately conscripted 500 men to join the forces already in the field. Of these, Connecticut supplied 200, of which 40 were Mohicans, while Massachusetts, with a much larger population, supplied 300.

Captain Samuel Mosely's Volunteers and two militia

companies commanded by Captain Daniel Henchman and Major John Pynchon, who had succeeded Simon Willard as Commander-in-Chief of the western forces, were now joined by Major Robert Treat and Captains Robert Seely and Thomas Watts of Connecticut, and Captains Thomas Lathrop of Beverly and Richard Beers of Watertown. The Commissioners ordered Pynchon to use Hadley as his headquarters, and to keep most of his troops quartered in that town.

MORE CHRISTIAN INDIAN BRAVERY

The soldiers involved in the Mount Hope campaign in the latter part of June were accompanied by three Natick Indians—Thomas Quannapowitt, James Quannapowitt, and Zachary Abram—who served as guides and scouts for the company led by Captain Thomas Prentice. That they were chosen for this extremely hazardous duty was in large part due to Daniel Gookin, who pleaded with Governor Leverett to make full use of their talents, among which he stressed those pertaining to guerilla warfare. At no time did these three men betray Gookin's trust, and they were so loyal to the English that they are credited with saving the company from being destroyed on more than one occasion. In spite of this, the soldiers were convinced that the Naticks were secretly allied with Philip, were in constant communication with his forces, and would eventually lead them into an ambush.

Ignoring his men's demands that he send the Naticks back to Boston, Prentice wrote such glowing reports about their bravery and faithfulness that the Council on July 2 commissioned Gookin to raise a company of 52 men. Gookin acted quickly. He formed a company in three days, and on July 6 they were sent to Mount Hope where they served under Captain Daniel Henchman. He released half of them after 25 days, but kept the others until he abandoned his pursuit of Philip's forces and returned to Boston. The Indians acquitted themselves bravely throughout the entire campaign. They suffered a number of casualties, proving that they exposed themselves to danger as readily as any other soldiers. Numbered among those killed was the 86-year-old Job Nesutan, Eliot's faithful servant, who was killed the day after he arrived at the front.

STRANGE MILITARY JUSTICE

When the first group of Indians was sent back to Boston

on July 31, they camped near a tavern the first night. While the men were resting from their long, hot march, one of them, known now only as Tom, asked permission to go into the nearby woods to cut a handle for his hatchet. When he failed to return after a reasonable length of time, six men were sent to look for him, but although they found his knife and hatchet, they were unable to find him, and another six men were sent to look for him, again with no success. Some of his comrades were now afraid that he had been killed by hostile Indians who were trailing them, but while they were discussing this supposition, Tom staggered toward them. He was so obviously drunk that his comrades' concern turned to anger. They tied him up then discussed the punishment he should receive. Since he had brought dishonor to their company, they decided he would have to die. When they told Tom their decision, he began to shout for help, and three of the officers came to his rescue.

Taken before the company commander for questioning, he admitted that he had bought a bottle of liquor from the tavern keeper when they first arrived. He hid it in his knapsack, then asked for permission to cut a handle for his hatchet so he could be alone to enjoy it. At first, he was going to remain in the woods until morning, reasoning that his extended absence would be excused since the company was being sent to Boston to be discharged. When the bottle was empty, however, he returned to buy another one, and it was then that his comrades had tried to execute him. He told the captain that he was much more concerned with the reactions of the other Indians than he was with those of his officers.

He soon learned that he had made a very serious error in judgment, for the captain told Tom that he would have to die for deserting his company in time of war, a punishment he hoped would serve as an example to the others. Although Tom was shocked by the severe sentence, he finally stated that he was ready to die, but only if he were executed in a military manner. He was afraid that if he was turned over to the men, they would torture him before they killed him. The captain agreed, and Tom was shot by a firing squad the following morning.

THE NATICKS ARE INTERNED ON DEER ISLAND

The patriot Indian forces were so successful during the first few months of the war that many of the colonists were convinced they were unbeatable. By the end of the summer, the sound of Philip's name was enough to send some of the more timorous into a state of near panic, and it was inevitable that this fear would eventually be accompanied by an equally-intense hatred directed against all Indians, either friendly or hostile. Emotions rose to such a fever pitch that Governor Leverett wisely disbanded the companies comprised mainly of Christian Indians. He then closed up two of the Praying Indian villages, and divided those who lived in them among the other five—Natick, Punkapoag, Nashoba, Wamesit, and Okkomakamesitt—so they could more easily be kept under surveillance. He also banned these Indians from visiting any of the English settlements. In spite of this, there were persistent rumors that a number of Praying Indians had taken part in raids against some of the frontier towns, and the Council reacted by decreeing that the Christian Indians could no longer travel more than one mile from their village unless they were accompanied by an Englishman. All Indians were to be regarded as hostiles, and could be shot on sight by the English.

Realizing that this would practically shut them off from all contact with the colonists, Eliot and Gookin pleaded with the Governor to send at least one Englishman to live at each of the villages. Although he agreed to do so, he found it virtually impossible to find anyone who would willingly accept this duty. The case of John Watson, Sr. of Cambridge, an inveterate Indian hater, illustrates why this was so. He was so certain that the Naticks were somehow involved in the rebellion that he went to live with them so he could more easily detect any of their subversive activities. After observing them closely for some time, he became convinced that they were a deeply religious people who wanted nothing more than to live at peace with the English, but when he explained his changed feelings to his friends, they bitterly accused him of being either a fool or a traitor—or both.

By the end of September, the settlers living near Natick met frequently to discuss how they should resolve the problem posed by the Naticks. There were those among them who believed that the Naticks were responsible for burning an old empty barn in Dedham, and they were certain that this was merely the first in a series of actions contemplated by these Indians. Although the authorities refused to believe this, they were forced to accept the fact that the Indians were in an extremely dangerous position. Since the colony could not spare any soldiers to keep them under constant protection, the only sensible alternative seemed to be to relocate them where they would be safe from attack, and Gookin was ordered to move them to Deer Island in Boston Harbor where they would be interned for the duration of the war. Within an hour after the order was received, they were on their way, escorted by a troop under Captain Thomas Prentice, who had volunteered the services of his men to protect them. The Indians were led to the waterfront, where a flotilla of boats ferried them to their new home.

Within minutes after they left Natick, a large group of their English neighbors swooped down on the village. When they saw that their intended victims were gone, they stole everything of value that had been left behind, including food supplies, furniture, guns, ammunition, hunting gear, and clothing, none of which was ever recovered by their owners.

THE WAMESITS ARE QUESTIONED IN BOSTON

The Wamesits suffered almost as much as the Naticks during these trying times. Some of their English neighbors tried to force them from their village by spreading false rumors about them, and when this did not have the desired effect, they committed several acts of vandalism which they blamed on the Indians, hoping that the authorities would remove them from their lands and open them to English occupancy.

Those of the English who remained friendly with the Wamesits cautioned them to ignore these happenings and continue with their daily routines, advice they were only too glad to accept. Their troubles with the settlers were compounded by the fact that the patriot Indians also hoped to discredit them with the authorities, and they too committed minor hostile acts in the communities near Wamesit so that public sentiment against the Praying Indians would be so high that they would be forced to join Philip to protect themselves. On October 18, when the English frenzy was at or near its peak, a small band of Nipmucks set fire to a haystack belonging to Lieutenant James Richardson, a close friend of the Wamesits. Although the damage was comparatively slight, the fire created the dramatic effect desired by those who had set it, for the nearby settlers, afraid that this was only the opening salvo in an all-out war against them, petitioned the General Court to rid the community of its unwanted

Indian neighbors. Lieutenant Richardson, the only man to speak in their defense, testified that the Wamesits had never committed any crimes against the English, and that the fires had been set by Philip's men. In spite of his testimony the Court sent a company of soldiers to Chelmsford to escort the Wamesits to Boston for questioning. Since the residents in and about Canton had made similar complaints against the Punkapoags, these Indians were also taken to Boston about the same time.

The soldiers arrived at Wamesit on October 21, ordered the Indians to tear the village down, and then herded them toward Boston, heavily burdened with their possessions. They had gone only a short distance when a messenger arrived with orders to send the women and children back to Wamesit since the authorities had been unable to find accommodations for the entire tribe. The men, about 33 in number, continued on toward Boston, and were placed under guard in Charlestown's town house, where they remained until the Court was ready to question them. After an investigation that continued for several days, the Court was unable to find any reason to keep them any longer, and allowed them to return home.

The Punkapoags were treated in approximately the same manner. Enroute to Boston, the women and children were ordered back to their village, while the men were taken to Dorchester where they were housed during their interrogation. After several days of intensive questioning, they, too, were released, and allowed to return home.

While the Wamesits were still being questioned, another barn was burned in Chelmsford by the patriot Indians. Although there were no adult males left at Wamesit, some of the nearby settlers blamed them for setting the fire, and decided to take the law into their own hands. They formed a vigilante committee, attacked the defenseless villagers while they slept, and killed one young boy and wounded five women, one of whom was the boy's mother. The General Court immediately ordered an investigation of the incident, and the two men responsible for the actual killing were arrested and tried for murder. In apite of the overwhelming evidence against them, the jury refused to find them guilty, and the men were set free.

THE WAMESITS FLEE TO PENNACOOK

By this time the Wamesit men had returned to their

village. They were so disheartened by the finding of the jury that some of them went to Mount Wachusett to join Philip's army, while the rest went to Pennacook (Concord, N.H.) where they were welcomed by Wannalancet, who had succeeded his father as Great Sachem of the Pawtucket Federation.

Pressed by John Eliot and Daniel Gookin, the Council sent messengers to the Wamesits, asking them to reconsider their action. Numphow, the leader of the Wamesits, told the messengers that he was concerned for the safety of his people, and that he was certain it would be better for them to live among the French in Canada than in the Massachusetts Bay Colony. Realizing that this would be construed by the Anglican Bishops as another victory by the French Catholics over the English Protestants, the Council redoubled its efforts to win him over. They promised that every precaution possible would be taken to protect his people if they returned to Wamesit, and Numphow, finally convinced of their sincerity, agreed to try living among the English again.

In spite of the Council's good intentions, the Wamesits continued to receive almost-daily threats against their lives during the next few months, and Numphow was at last forced to petition the General Court to remove them to a safer area. Although the Court agreed to honor his request, it became concerned with matters of so much more pressing concern that it did not act on his petition at once. Realizing that any further delay might cost him the lives of many of his people, Numphow led them back to Pennacook, leaving Wamesit under cover of darkness. Because of the extreme cold, the distance involved, and the need to travel as swiftly as possible, Numphow left six of his oldest men and women behind. Three were blind, and all were so weak that they would have had to be carried almost the entire distance, an extra burden that would have slowed the entire group to such an extent that the dangers they already faced would be increased immeasurably. Their families refused to abandon them in this fashion until Numphow convinced them that even the most virulent Indian hater would not harm them since they were so completely helpless. In this, he miscalculated the temper of the nearby settlers, for when they learned that the Wamesits were gone, a group of them went to the village to scavenge whatever valuables might have been left behind. When they discovered the old people, they herded them together in one of the wigwams, sealed the entrance, then set the dwelling afire, deliberately burning them to death.

In the meanwhile, the refugees sped toward Pennacook, driven by the fear that they would be hunted down and killed as soon as the English learned they were gone. They stayed well away from the more highly-travelled trails to minimize the danger of being accidentally discovered, thereby adding to the rigors of the flight. Before they finally arrived at their destination, they were so debilitated by the lack of food, the pace they tried to maintain, and their exposure to the numbing cold that a large number of them died, one of the first to succumb being Numphow, their aged leader.

THE PUNKAPOAGS ARE INTERNED AT DEER ISLAND

The Punkapoags returned to their village after being assured by the authorities that they would no longer be molested by their neighbors. These were well-meant but empty promises, for the settlers continued to harass them so much that Eliot and Gookin became concerned for their safety, and petitioned the Court to send them to Deer Island for protection. Prior to the war, this island was used to pasture sheep, and under normal conditions could easily sustain a few families for an indefinite period of time. These were not normal times, however, for the advent of the Punkapoags swelled the population of the already over-crowded island to more than 400 men, women, and children, all of whom were forced to exist as best they could on the available fish and shellfish. Eliot and Gookin visited their charges whenever possible, always bringing with them as much food and warm clothing as they could beg or buy, but in spite of their efforts, many of the Indians were unable to survive their enforced stay on the island. The two men were themselves the target of a large number of threats, and even several attempts on their lives. Gookin was especially hated because he was Irish, and there were rumors that he was a Catholic and in the employ of foreign interests. Eliot's calling and long, blameless past did not save him from being almost equally suspect, and on one of their trips to Deer Island, their boat and supplies they were carrying were lost when they were deliberately rammed by another boat. The two men spent some time in the water, and were saved from drowning only by the quick action of some friends who had witnessed the entire scene.

THE NIPMUCKS ATTACK HASSANAMESSIT

In November, a large force of Nipmucks attacked the Praying Indian village of Hassanamessit, taking more than 200 prisoners with them when they finally left. Only a short time before this, the English had disarmed these Indians for security reasons, and had treated them so abominably in the process that some of the more reasonable settlers were afraid that the soldiers had created a rupture between the two people which might never heal. There was at least a bit of truth in this, for when the Nipmucks attacked the village, most of the Praying Indians hailed them as liberators, and left with them without putting up even a token struggle. They did not all react in this way, for there were those who defended themselves and their families with sticks, stones, and hastily fashioned war clubs, and some of these men even managed to fight their way to safety. Job Kattenanit was one of these, but he was the only member of his family to escape, for his three children were taken prisoner. When he arrived at Mendon, Gookin gave him a safe-conduct pass so he could go to Mount Wachusett to arrange for his family's ransom. He had gone only a short distance when he was captured by a group of Captain Daniel Henchman's soldiers. They stripped him of his clothing, gun, ammunition, and other personal belongings, then brought him before their captain. Henchman was convinced that the pass was genuine, but he was afraid that his men would rebel if he set the Indian free, so he sent him to Boston where he was thrown into a small cell that was overcrowded before he arrived. He remained there for three weeks, then was taken to Deer Island where he was interned with the other Praying Indians.

SAMUEL MOSELY AND HIS VOLUNTEERS

Captain Samuel Mosely, a cousin of Governor John Leverett, proved to be one of the most implacable enemies the Indians had during the King Philip War. An unconventional man, he first came to public notice before the war when he was granted a commission as a Privateer to fight against the Spanish in the West Indies. Within a short time, he returned to Boston with two enemy ships he had captured.

He made so much money from his brief stint as a legal pirate that he used some of it to buy more ships. These he rented to the colony when the authorities gathered an armada to protect merchant shipping from three Dutch pirates who were operating off the coast of Massachusetts. Mosely was in personal command of one of these ships, and within a short time he returned to Boston with the captured Dutchmen. The pirates were tried in Boston, and while most of them were released because of the lack of evidence, five were found guilty and sentenced to be hanged. The war broke out just before their executions were to take place, and the sentences were never carried out.

Mosely's success in capturing the pirates had made him one of the most popular men in the colony, and a group of his admirers easily persuaded him to take an active part in the war against the Indians. Since he had never held a military office, he was not allowed to take command of any of the militia companies, but he was granted permission to form and lead a company of volunteers. Such was the extent of his popularity that 110 men signed the articles that formally made them a part of his company within three hours after his call for volunteers was posted. Among these were a number of his former crew members, some of the pirates who had been released because of lack of evidence against them, and the five men who were waiting to be executed. These last were pardoned when they volunteered to serve with Mosely for the duration of the war.

Those of his men who owned dogs were encouraged to bring them on the expedition, for Mosely knew of the part they had played in Virginia in hunting down rebellious Indians during the early years. The dogs proved to be invaluable, for Mosely used them to track down Indians hiding in the swamps, and as a psychological weapon to force information from prisoners who could not be intimidated by conventional methods.

Mosely and his company served throughout the war with varying degrees of success, and although he cannot be considered the most effective soldier in the colonial army, he was one of the most colorful. Shortly after Captain Hutchinson was killed at Wickabaug Pond, Mosely's men captured two Indians with the aid of their dogs. When they were questioned, the men first refused to talk, but when the soldiers threatened to unloose the dogs on them, the Indians admitted thtat they had taken part in the ambush. Once he had extracted this information from them, Mosely dragged them to the edge of the woods, and shot each of them through the back of the head.

On August 22, Mosely was marching his men toward Wamesit to interrogate Wannalancet when he learned that

Lancaster had been attacked the day before. He decided to postpone his visit to Wamesit until a later date, then raced back to Lancaster where he was told that there was evidence to suspect that some of the Hassanamessits living at Okkommakamesit had been involved in the attack. He hurried to the village to investigate the matter, and while there, he saw 15 Hassanamessits taking part in a ceremonial dance. Mistaking it for a victory dance to celebrate the success of the Lancaster raid, he placed them under arrest, then searched their effects for any evidence that might help to incriminate them. The fact that he found a small quantity of slugs, powder, and bullets convinced him they were guilty. Another Praying Indian named David was also questioned while the search was being conducted, the he told the soldiers that the 15 men were among those who had participated in the Lancaster raid. Mosely manacled them, kept them together with a long rope that was passed around the neck of each man, then marched them to Boston under a strong guard.

When they were questioned by the authorities, four of the men were immediately released, while the other 11 were found innocent after a short trial. The authorities next questioned David, and he at last admitted that his accusations were false. He explained that when Mosely's men first arrived at Marlborough, they tied him to a tree, and threatened to kill him if he did not confess that he had taken part in the raid. Only a short time before this, his brother Andrew had been executed as a spy by the English soldiers, and although the Praying Indians knew he was innocent, none had stepped forward to speak in his defense because they feared to do anything that might arouse the anger or suspicions of Mosely's wild men. David knew why they had kept quiet, for he had kept silent for the same reason. Perversely, he still blamed them for his brother's death, and he decided to save his own life as well as avenge his brother's death by accusing them.

The members of the Court were understandably annoyed when he completed his confession, and when they were told that he had once shot and wounded a young boy who was tending sheep in Marlborough, they sentenced him to be sold to the West Indies as a slave.

The 15 Hassanamessits were ordered interned on Deer Island for the remainder of the war, but eight of these men managed to escape before they were taken there, taking with them a number of other Indians who were waiting to be tried on various charges. Afraid they would be executed if they were recaptured, they travelled to Mount Wachusett where they joined Philip's army.

AN INDIAN IS EXECUTED ON BOSTON COMMON

When it became generally known throughout Boston that a large number of Indians had escaped from jail, several men banded together to storm the jail and administer their own brand of justice to those who were left. None of the men would accept the role of leader, and they at last decided to offer this honor to Captain James Oliver, one of the men serving on the jury in the Indian trials. They arrived at his home late at night, and when they told him the nature of their errand, Oliver became so enraged that he drove them from his house with his cane.

He reported the incident to the Governor the following morning, and the two men discussed the matter at length. They realized that the temper of the people was such that other, even more serious, incidents might occur if something drastic was not done, and they at last decided to hang one of the prisoners, hoping that his death would appease the mob, and thereby save the others. They ordered the High Sheriff to surrender one of the prisoners to the mob so they could execute him, themselves.

When this was done, the men tied a noose about the poor man's neck, then led him swiftly to the Common where the rope was tossed over the limb of a large tree. A number of the men grabbed the loose end, then hoisted the Indian into the air. Before he strangled, they lowered him to the ground, revived him, then hoisted him into the air, again. They repeated this four times, and might have continued on throughout the rest of the day but for another Indian, who mercifully plunged his knife into the victim's chest, thereby ending his suffering.

MOSELY DESTROYS TWO OF WANNALANCET'S VILLAGES

Shortly after the Hassanamessits left for Boston, Mosely learned of the raid that took place at Springfield on August 24, and he rushed to that town as quickly as possible. Arriving long after Muttawmp had left, he sent his men out to scour the surrounding countryside for stragglers, and they

returned with an old squaw who was questioned closely by
Mosely. She told him that Philip, with a force of 600 men,
was planning to attack three border towns simultaneously in
the very near future, and that Philip was building a fortified
village near Mount Wachusett in which he and his people
intended to spend the winter. When she told him that this
was all she knew, Mosely turned her over to his men who
brought her to a nearby field where she was literally torn to
pieces by their dogs.

In a letter to Governor John Leverett after this incident,
Mosely stated, "...I desire to be excused if my tongue or my
pen outrun my wit, being in a passion...Seeing what mischief
has been done by the Indians, which I have been eyewitness
to, would make a wiser person than I am willing to have
revenge of any of them."

For some weeks before the raid at Lancaster, he had
received reports that a large body of Indians was camped on
the Merrimack River near Chelmsford. That these were
Wannalancet's people, all of whom had been converted to
Christianity, meant nothing to Mosely, for he found it almost
impossible to distinguish between a friendly and a hostile
Indian. After he sent the Hassanamesits to Boston, he led the
rest of his company to Chelmsford where he hoped to
eliminate the threat these Indians posed to the well-being of
the colony. A few months earlier, when Wannalancet first
learned of the outbreak of hostilities, he abandoned his village
in Chelmsford, and retired to another on the Merrimack
River in Concord, New Hampshire, so that his people would
not become involved on either side. Misunderstanding the
reason for this move, the authorities were afraid that he intended to join Philip. They sent him several messages ex-
pressing the hope that the friendship that had been maintained between the English and the Pawtuckets through the
years would never be broken, and they urged him to send six
representatives to meet with Daniel Gookin and John Eliot to
draw up a treaty that would guarantee the continuation of this
friendship.

Wannalancet was convinced that the English were sincere,
so he began to move back to Pawtucket Falls. On the way,
however, his scouts brought disquieting news that Mosely was
also heading for the same destination, and he returned to
Pennacook. Wannalancet was only too aware of Mosely's
attitude toward all Indians, and he knew that an apology
from the Massachusetts governor, regardless of how sincere it

might be, would not bring back to life those of his people that Mosely might kill.

When the soldiers arrived at the deserted village at Pawtucket Falls, they looted all the valuables they could carry with them, burned the village to the ground, then set out after the fugitives. Wannalancet's scouts spotted them long before they arrived at Pennacook, and Wannalancet abandoned this village, too, and drifted deeper into the woods. When the troopers arrived at the village, Mosely ordered all the food supplies destroyed, then burned this village to the ground, also. Although the Pawtuckets watching from the forest wanted to attack the soldiers, Wannalancet restrained them.

The authorities were again outraged when they learned of Mosely's latest exploit, but his close relationship to the Governor and his great popularity with the people prevented them from censuring him publicly as they might have wished. Instead, they sent another apology to Wannalancet, reaffirming their desire to remain at peace with the Pawtuckets.

THE NASHOBAS ARE INTERNED ON DEER ISLAND

Throughout the first months of the war, the Nashoba Indians were under constant pressure to join Philip, but although they refused to do so, their English neighbors did not trust them. Some of these settlers, envious of the way in which the community had thrived, openly talked of confiscating their well-tended lands, and they petitioned the authorities to have the Nashobas driven from their village. The Indians were fortunate in that they were under the protection of John Hoare, the minister of the Concord Church, for he had enough influence to offset almost every scheme that was advanced to discredit or harm them.

Some of the settlers, knowing that Mosely would believe anything told him about the Indians, enlisted his aid by informing him that the Nashobas were secretly allied with Philip. They told him that although they gave every outward appearance of being peaceful and industrious, they regularly joined the marauders roaming the nearby countryside at night, and had taken part in a number of attacks against the border settlements. Mosely was convinced these stories were true, and on the following Sunday morning, he and his men went to the village and surrounded the meetinghouse where the Nashobas were attending services that were being conducted by Mr. Hoare. When these were ended, he strode to the pulpit, and announced that the village was under martial law, and that everyone was to be ready to go to Boston the following morning.

Throughout the rest of the day, Mosely's men visited each home to appropriate for themselves all the valuables owned by the Indians. Some even stripped the meetinghouse of a number of religious articles in spite of Mr. Hoare's vehément protests. When Mosely appeared in Boston with his prisoners, the members of the Court were in turn amazed and dismayed, afraid that it presaged a complete takeover of civil authority by the military. Unwilling to run counter to public sentiment which still held him in high esteem, they did not reprimand him. Even when several of the leading citizens of Concord attested to the loyalty of the Nashobas, the General Court refused to take any action that might be construed as a censure of the popular Mosely. Instead, they sent the Nashobas to Deer Island where they helped to swell the population of the already-overcrowded island, and Mosely was allowed to return to his duties in the field.

More than 500 men, women, and children were on the island during the winter of 1675-1676, one of the longest and coldest winters in colonial history. Despite the efforts of Eliot and Gookin, a large number of the ill-clothed, ill-housed, and ill-fed Indians died before spring finally arrived. Although almost every citizen in the colony knew of their suffering, there were a large number who felt they were being treated far too leniently, and they circulated petitions demanding that the internees either be executed or sold into slavery. When the members of the General Court learned of this petition, they at last took a courageous stand by declaring that the Praying Indians, on the basis of the treaties signed by their fathers in 1644, were allies of the colony, and, as such, under the protection of its Government. This ruling saved the Indians from certain massacre, for a group of Bostonians were planning to attack the island and kill its unarmed occupants, and only the threat of retaliation by the colony's armed forces prevented them from carrying out their plan.

THE NORWOTTOCKS ABANDON THEIR VILLAGE

In July, the soldiers stationed at Hadley confiscated 29 guns from the Norwottucks, a relatively small tribe living between Hadley and Northampton. The guns were later returned when the leaders of the tribe promised to join the

English in their war against Philip. They were given an opportunity to prove their loyalty by sending a contingent of warriors to help the English soldiers who were sent to search for the Quaboags after the Brookfield attack, and 30 warriors from the tribe volunteered to accompany the soldiers. Their conduct in this search left so much to be desired that when they returned, the citizens of Hadley met with the Council to discuss their future relations with them. Several points were raised, one being that this year the Indians had not asked for permission to plant their crops until the spring, the first time this had ever happened, for they usually asked during the winter. This clearly indicated that they knew of Philip's plans long before the war began. Another was the Norwottuck's attitude during the recent search for the Quaboags. Although they had accompanied the soldiers, they did not volunteer any information that could be used to find their quarry, and they told the English that if they did find the Quaboags they could not fight against them, for their laws forbade them to wage war against those with the close blood ties that existed between the two tribes.

A short time before the meeting was held, word was received that Sagamore Sam had led a small raiding party against the town of Lancaster where he killed a family of four as they worked in their fields. When news of this reached Hadley, both the civil and military leaders decided that the Norwottuck village should again be searched for firearms as a precautionary measure.

Captains Watts, Lathrop, and Beers held a council of war to determine how to stage the disarmament proceedings, and they agreed there would be less chance of untoward incidents if it was held in conjunction with the soldiers stationed at the Northampton garrison. They sent a messenger to that town to advise them of their plans, stating that if the Northampton soldiers entered the village from the south while they entered from the north, none of the Indians would be able to escape.

Another messenger was sent to the Norwottucks to explain what was expected of them, and shortly after the messenger returned from his assignment, an old Sachem came to the garrison to speak with the English leaders. He told them that most of the older men in the tribe joined him in the hope that they might continue to live in peace with the English as they had for so many years, and they were anxious to prove their loyalty by cooperating with them in any way possible. The younger men, however, refused to part with their weapons. He was certain that if the English tried to disarm them by force, the young men would resist, and go to war against them. When the English refused to withdraw their demands, the old man sorrowfully returned to his village, promising that he would try to convince the young men to change their attitudes.

Another messenger was sent to the Norwottucks for their answer, but he was told that the entire tribe would vote on the matter when they assembled that night. He returned to the village late in the evening, but he was now greeted with threats and jostled about by a group of the younger men, and he sped back to the garrison, without waiting for a reply, afraid they intended to kill him.

At the Council Fires, a young warrior pleaded with his comrades to resist the demands of the English. He warned them they had very little time to waste in debating the issue, for the English soldiers were sure to appear in the morning. He could see no reason for a debate, however, for they had only two courses to choose from—they could agree to the English demands, or they could abandon their village, and join the patriot Indian army. If the English treated them as they had other tribes in the past, they could expect other demands would follow after they surrendered their guns, demands that would not only strip them of their dignity as men, but quite possibly of their identity as Norwottucks, as well.

The old Sachem rose to speak when the younger man had finished. He warned that there were too many Englishmen and too few Indians to carry out a successful rebellion, and he asked them to remember the many years in which the two people had lived together in peace. He was certain that if the Indians were patient, the era of mutual understanding would continue. A fiery young warrior shouted that the English were living on lands they had stolen from the Indians, and that the Indians were now forced to farm these lands on shares or go without food. When the old Sachem tried to answer him, the young man stepped forward and killed him with his tomahawk.

No further discussion was needed. The women and children gathered all the food and personal effects they could carry, then the entire tribe abandoned the village.

THE NORWOTTUCKS JOIN THE PATRIOT INDIAN FORCES

When the messenger returned to Hadley, the three captains agreed that they would have to disarm the Norwottucks by force, and they marched to the Indian village the following morning with their entire command. Their show of force was unnecessary, however, for they found the fort completely deserted except for the body of the old Sachem. Lathrop and Beers quickly mustered a company of 100 men to chase after the fleeing Indians, and sent the rest of the soldiers back to garrison.

Since the Indians were forced to travel slowly because of their heavily burdened women and children, the soldiers caught up with them several miles beyond Hatfield, at a place known as Sugar-Loaf Hill.

To give their women and children time in which to get a safe distance away, 40 of the warriors waited in ambush for the English. The Indians opened fire when the soldiers were in the trap, killing several of them. Once the survivors were over their initial shock, they took cover, and fought back bravely, although with little or no effect since the Indians were careful not to expose themselves to their fire. At the end of three hours, the Indians were certain that their families were far enough away from their pursuers, and they drifted off into the forest, leaving nine of the English lying dead on the battlefield.

The Norwottucks continued on to the Indian village at Deerfield where they were warmly welcomed by the Pocumtucks. On September 1st, a joint expedition of the two tribes attacked the Deerfield garrison, and met with very little resistance as they set fire to most of the houses in the town before they returned to their village. The following day, they attacked the Squakeag (Northfield) garrison while most of the people were at work in the fields. They killed eight of the settlers, burned many of the houses, slaughtered all the livestock, and destroyed most of the crops before they finally left.

By coincidence, while this raid was taking place Captain Beers was in Hadley working on plans to evacuate the Northfield settlers, and the following day, still unaware of what had taken place, he led 36 troopers to Northfield. With him were a number of civilian teamsters who were driving the oxcarts that were to be used in the evacuation. Because he had to slow his pace to accommodate the slower moving oxen, he was still several miles from his destination when night fell. He continued on until he reached a field that adjoined a small brook, a site he considered ideal for his purposes since there was ample grazing for the animals, could be defended easily, and was only three miles from the town.

In the morning, Beers and his men continued on to Northfield on foot, leaving their horses at the campsite. As they neared the town, they were forced to wade across a small brook that cut through the main road. While they were crossing, they were attacked by a band of Indians. Captain Beers and 18 of his troopers were killed immediately, and the rest of the men raced back to the campsite without firing a shot. There, they mounted their horses, and fled back to Hadley. Most of the survivors reached the garrison before dark, while two others staggered in the next day, and a third man arrived two days after the ambush. This man claimed he had been taken prisoner by the Indians who brought him back to their village to torture him. While his captors were celebrating their victory, a Natick Indian crept into the camp, cut his bonds, led him to safety, and then disappeared before the Englishman could learn who he was. A fourth soldier stumbled into Hadley five days later. He had eaten nothing for three days, and was so shaken by the horrors of the ambush that he could remember nothing that had happened to him since then.

Major Treat, on a routine patrol with a company of 100 Connecticut troopers, arrived at Hadley on September 3rd, and he was ordered to go to Northfield to attempt another evacuation of the town. On the evening of September 5, he camped in almost the same place that Captain Beers and his men had a few days earlier. The following morning, as he travelled toward Northfield, he came to an open field where the Indians had driven 20 poles into the ground and stuck the heads of the dead troopers on them. After he buried all the bodies he could find into a common grave, he continued on to the town where he ordered every available person to help in the evacuation. Shortly before he was ready to leave, his scouts returned with the disquieting news that they had seen several bands of Indians near the village. So that he would lose as little time as possible, he would not allow the settlers to bury the eight men who had been killed in the fields, nor would he encumber himself with any of the livestock, but left them all behind.

As he reached the outskirts of the town, he was attacked by a small band of Indians. They fired one volley at him, then immediately returned to the safety of the forest. The soldiers formed into ranks to fight off another attack, but the Indians did not reappear. When some time passed with no further sign of the enemy, Treat resumed the march to Hadley. Because he feared that the Indians had gone for reinforcements, he drove his men at top speed all the way, and they reached Hadley that same evening.

Only 14 Indians had participated in the ambush on the Connecticut troopers. After the initial attack, they prudently withdrew deep into the forest until they were certain the soldiers would not return, then entered the town, and drove the livestock to their fortress where they held a huge feast to celebrate their latest victory over the English. Bands of Indians continued to visit the deserted town until they had plundered from it everything of value they could carry away with them, after which, they burned the town to the ground.

DEERFIELD ATTACKED BY A SMALL BAND OF INDIANS

On September 12, about a week before the western army was reinforced, a small band of Indians attacked a group of 22 heavily-armed settlers at Deerfield as they were passing from one garrison to another to attend church services. Although the Indians were driven off after a brief skirmish, they managed to burn two more houses, and captured 30 horses as well as several wagonloads of beef and pork before they left. They also captured one of the settlers, and brought him to their camp where they tortured and then killed him.

News of his capture so infuriated the soldiers that a number of them volunteered to search for the Indians who had taken part in the raid. They marched to Deerfield more than 48 hours after the attack, and spent two whole days vainly patrolling the nearby hills for signs of the Indians who had long since retired to their fort. Tired and discouraged from their futile search, the soldiers returned to Deerfield.

MUTTAWMP DESTROYS LATHROP'S COMPANY

In spite of the constant threat of Indian attack, the Deerfield settlers managed to harvest their crops by September 18. That they were able to accomplish this was mainly due to the fact that the reinforcements from Massachusetts and Connecticut allowed Major Pynchon to send Captain

Mosely's company to Deerfield to protect the settlers as they worked in the fields. This was an unusually large crop, and extremely valuable in light of the tons of food stuff that had been destroyed by the Indians throughout the summer. For this reason, Major Pynchon wanted most of it brought to Hadley so he could disburse it to those communities that would need it throughout the winter. When the produce was packed into wagons and ready for the trip to Hadley, Captain Lathrop's company was sent to Deerfield to convoy the wagon train, thus freeing Mosely's men to patrol the nearby forests for signs of Indian war parties.

Lathrop was not a strict disciplinarian, and his men were completely relaxed on the march to Hadley. Since it was an unseasonably warm day, most of them even threw their outer clothing and guns on the wagons while they roamed about looking for clusters of sweet wild grapes to slake their thirst. When the advance escort of the wagon train arrived at Muddy Brook (now called Bloody Brook) in South Deerfield, they found their way blocked by a number of huge trees that the Indians had felled across the road. This obvious guerilla tactic should have alerted them to the possibility of danger, but they merely cleared the road, then sat down to rest while they waited for the slow-moving wagons to catch up with them.

Muttawmp was as anxious to have the newly-harvested grain as Pynchon, and he and approximately 200 warriors were hidden nearby, waiting to ambush the wagon train. When the greater part of the soldiers arrived at the place he had selected for the ambush, his men attacked. They did this so swiftly and efficiently that most of the soldiers, including Captain Lathrop, were killed within minutes. Those who survived the initial attack, scrambled about to arm themselves, then fought back desperately, but to no avail, for they, too, were soon dead. The only ones who escaped the slaughter were a small number of troopers and teamsters who had lagged far behind the rest of the company.

The victorious Indians first stripped the dead of any valuables they were carrying, then turned their attention to the wagons. They cut open bags of grain and a number of feather beds, and scattered their contents about in the wind. As they were engaged in these childish acts of destruction, Captain Samuel Mosely and his 70 troopers appeared on the scene, drawn there by the sounds of the guns. He charged the Indians, recklessly, but retreated when two of his men were killed and a number of others were wounded in the attack.

The Indian leaders were well aware of Mosely's hatred of their people, a hatred so intense that it bordered on pathomania, and seeing that he refused to continue the fight, Monoco taunted him, saying "Come, Mosely, come! You seek Indians, you want Indians; here is Indians enough for you." Mosely's pride would not let him leave after this, and he engaged the Indians in a fight that lasted from noon until dusk, when he again ordered his men to retreat. Minutes after he withdrew, Major Treat appeared with a company of 100 soldiers and 60 Mohicans. The Nipmucks were now greatly out-numbered, and slipped away into the forest where the troopers did not dare follow.

The soldiers gathered their wounded, and returned to Deerfield where they rested through the night. The following day, Treat returned to the battlefield to conduct funeral services for the 71 men who had been killed, then buried them all in a common grave.

COLONIAL MORALE AT A VERY LOW POINT

Civilian morale, extremely low since the start of the war, sank to new depths when news of the massacre at Bloody Brook reached Boston. The colonists were so far removed from the front that the news that reached them was seldom completely accurate. Sometimes, many days elapsed with no news of any kind, and there were a large number who allowed their imaginations to fill the void. Some of the settlers were in a state of near-hysteria, and ready to believe even the most patently absurd stories and rumors. An example of this occurred in late summer after a violent storm raged along the Massachusetts coast. During the storm, a large number of ships were smashed together or driven aground, wharves were wrecked, houses destroyed, and huge stands of timber toppled over. An Indian prisoner told his guard that the storm had been sent by Hobbamocko who promised that each tree blown down by the gale foretold the death of an Englishman in the war. This story quickly circulated, and the more superstitious colonists believed it implicitly.

Included in this group were a number of people holding responsible positions of authority, who tried to avenge their real or imagined defeats by permitting acts of wanton cruelty to be committed on those Indians unfortunate enough to be captured and brought into Boston. Some were hanged in public ceremonies on the Common, while others were sold into slavery, many of them first undergoing the most cruel tortures their sadistic captors could devise.

Morale in the military was as bad as it was on the home front. Many soldiers wanted no more of the war, and were on the verge of mutiny. Those sent on patrol invariably remained close to the garrisons, unwilling to venture too deep into the forest for fear they would meet the enemy. The desertion rate was so high that every company was desperately in need of replacements, forcing both Connecticut and Massachusetts to step up their draft calls. They were unable to fill their quotas, however, for many of those who were drafted either hid in the woods or left New England entirely, and did not return until after they learned of Philip's death.

When Major Pynchon saw that the colonies were sending him only a small percentage of the men he needed, he closed the Deerfield garrison, moved the families living there to Hatfield, and apportioned the soldiers among the various companies to help bring them back as close to their normal strength as possible.

THE BRIEF NEUTRALITY OF THE AGAWAMS

By the middle of September, a large force of Nipmucks was camped on the western banks of the Connecticut River, a site that allowed them to harass the settlements of Hatfield and Northampton almost at will. Some of their raiding parties travelled as far south as Springfield, and most of the settlers in that town were so frightened that they would not leave their homes, even to attend church services, unless they were protected by a strong military escort.

To this time, Wequogon, Sachem of the Agawam (Springfield) Indians, had remained neutral, preferring to sit out the war in his fortified village on the east bank of the river rather than commit himself either to Philip or the English. The Springfield settlers refused to regard his people as anything but potential enemies, and they begged the military leaders to insure their neutrality by disarming them. After several meetings, they agreed to do this, but when the members of the Council at Hartford learned of the proposed action, they immediately sent word that they disapproved of it. They argued that the Indians needed their guns to provide food for their families, and confiscating them would antagonize them and drive them to Philip's side. They suggested that the Agawams be forced to surrender a number of their children as hostages, well aware that Indians loved their children so much they would do nothing that might endanger their safety, and they argued their case so effectively that the settlers in Springfield voted to adopt their plan.

Strangely enough, when the Agawams were told that they must surrender some of their children as a guarantee of their future good behavior, they agreed to do so with little or no apparent reluctance. The youngsters were immediately taken to Hartford where they were kept under constant guard during the first few days of their imprisonment. They were so well-behaved and posed so little threat to the safety of the English, that the close surveillance was relaxed, and the children were soon left alone for long periods of time.

In the meanwhile, Philip's messengers continued to press the Agawams to join the Great Fight, and after the attack on Springfield on September 26, the Agawams agreed to give Philip their active support. They first sent a small group of men to Hartford to rescue the children, and the colonists had so relaxed their vigilance by this time that the prisoners were easily freed. Elated by the ease with which they had carried out their assignment, the Agawams were unable to resist the temptation to boast of it when they stopped at a small Indian village near Windsor, and they also blurted out the fact that Springfield was to be destroyed on October 5th. One of the local Indians, a young man named Toto, was employed on a small farm in Windsor. He was so disturbed by this news that he immediately told his master of it, who, in turn sent a messenger to Springfield to alert the people to their danger.

THE NIPMUCKS ATTACK SPRINGFIELD

The Springfield attack was led by Muttawmp and Wequogon, who camouflaged their plans so well that the English had no inkling that Springfield was to be the Indians' next target. On the day before the scheduled raid, Wequogon led 200 warriors to a swamp about six miles north of Hadley where they moved about freely during the day to make certain they would be seen by the settlers. At dusk, they lighted a large number of campfires, and while most of the men returned to Agawam under cover of darkness, a small group remained behind to keep the fires burning throughout the night. Shortly before daybreak, this last group also returned to Agawam, leaving the campsite completely abandoned.

As Muttawmp had planned, the Hadley settlers, certain they would be attacked in the morning, sent an urgent appeal to Springfield for help, and most of the soldiers were sent to Hadley, leaving Springfield almost completely unprotected.

The message from Windsor did not arrive at Springfield until after midnight on October 5. Everyone in the settlement was immediately awakened, and herded together in three of the larger garrisons, while messengers were sent to Major Pynchon at Hadley and Major Treat at Westfield advising them of Springfield's danger.

The settlers remained awake throughout the rest of the long night, nervously awaiting the sounds that would signal the start of the attack. When this did not materialize by daybreak, they all sat down to breakfast, then attended religious services at the meetinghouse. After these were concluded, some of the more courageous men decided to resume their normal daily routines, convinced that the Indians did not intend to attack their town that day.

Lieutenant Thomas Cooper, who knew most of the Agawams intimately, was also skeptical about the accuracy of the information received from Windsor, and he volunteered to go to Agawam to see if the Indians had indeed become hostile.

Instead of forbidding him to take this senseless risk, the others encouraged him, and he and another young man named Thomas Miller saddled their horses and started on their journey. Less than 30 minutes later, Cooper's horse, carrying his lifeless body, galloped back to the town, closely followed by a band of shrieking Indians.

Major Treat arrived at Springfield several hours after the initial attack, and Muttawmp deployed a part of his army to drive him away from the town. Since Treat was so over-whelmingly outnumbered, he was forced to retreat to a position several miles from Springfield where he made his stand at the top of a small hill. Just as Muttawmp was ordering more warriors to aid those who surrounded Treat's troopers, Major Pynchon arrived with 200 soldiers, and Muttawmp was forced to retreat. He withdrew to a steep hill just outside the town, and he and his men celebrated their victory with a dance, then gorged themselves on the freshly-slaughtered cattle. At daybreak, the Indians retired to one of their forts approximately 50 miles north of Hadley. This was one of their most successful raids of the fall, for they succeeded in destroying 30 houses, 25 barns, several mills belonging to Major Pynchon, and almost all the buildings in which his servants were quartered.

Although Governor John Leverett and his Council had appointed Major John Pynchon Commander-in-Chief of the western campaign, Pynchon was unable to exercise absolute command of the Connecticut troops sent to him in September. Major Treat was certain that his authority was equal to that of Pynchon, and he invariably went on patrols without consulting Pynchon beforehand. The situation was not a happy one for Pynchon, but he refused to issue an ultimatum that might create a rift between the Massachusetts and Connecticut commands.

The situation came abruptly to a head on September 30, however, for on that day Major Treat and his entire command returned to Connecticut without asking for or receiving permission to do so after he received a message from Hartford ordering him to move his troops to Wethersfield where there were persistent rumors of an impending Indian attack.

The frustrated Pynchon immediately wrote to the Commissioners. He told them of Treat's absence, but did not elaborate on it. He also strongly urged them to reconsider their orders pertaining to keeping most of his soldiers at Hadley, for he believed that he could more effectively protect the settlements if a small garrison was permanently maintained in each one. These small units could easily withstand assaults by large hostile forces until outside help arrived.

Pynchon was one of the largest property owners in the Springfield area, and his prolonged absence at the front had caused him to suffer severe financial reverses. He asked to be relieved of his command so he could again look after his properties and suggested that Captain Samuel Appleton, one of the ablest officers in the field, replace him.

After the Springfield attack of October 5, the dispirited Pynchon sent another dispatch to the Commissioners. He stated that those of the Springfield settlers who lost their homes had already been taken in by other families, but while this solved one problem, it created another one just as serious. The shortage of food coupled with the crowded quarters made for such uncomfortable living conditions that the entire community was troubled by constant bickering. This condition was bound to get worse since the loss of the mills meant that there would soon be no more bread in the Springfield area.

He again recommended that the policy governing the prosecution of the war be changed, stating that a small permanent garrison in each settlement would be much more effective in combatting Indian attacks than the system being used.

He assured the Commissioners that he would not become lax while he waited to be relieved, but that he would continue to patrol the area every day. A few of the Connecticut men had returned to the front, but he complained that the continued absence of the greater part of Major Treat's force left him dangerously shorthanded. He closed by stating that although he had not yet received official notification that Captain Appleton was to relieve him, he would soon turn his command over to him.

Pynchon was formally relieved by Samuel Appleton on October 12. The younger officer had taken command of a highly-disorganized army where morale was so low that many of the men continued to desert, and the scouts still were afraid to venture very far from their garrisons when they were sent on patrol. Acting quickly to restore discipline, he ordered Captains Mosely and Seely to bring their companies to Hadley for permanent duty. Although Mosely obeyed him at once, Seely did not appear for several days, and when he did, he came alone. He explained that he had only an honorary commission from Connecticut, and could give no orders unless he was first authorized to do so by his superior officer, Major Treat.

Appleton, livid with rage, thundered that since he was Major Treat's superior officer, every man in the Connecticut force was subject to his orders. After the two had argued heatedly for some time, Seely at last agreed to bring his company to Hadley. Several days later, Appleton received a message from him saying that Major Treat had ordered him to remain where he was. Appleton considered this a treasonous action, and he dispatched a message to the Connecticut Council urging them to recall and court martial both Treat and Seely.

He then assembled his companies and marched them toward Northfield where he hoped to bring the war directly to the Indians. He had gone only a few miles when a scout reported that a large body of Indians was massed on the west banks of the river near Deerfield. He raced to Hatfield, then pressed on, hoping to arrive at Deerfield before the Indians dispersed. While he was on the march, a heavy rain began to fall, whipped by huge gusts of wind, and certain that the Indians would not attack any town until the weather had cleared, he returned to Hadley.

Late in the evening of October 16, he received an urgent appeal for help from the Northampton authorities who claimed there were strong indications they would be attacked on the following day. Less than an hour later, another message arrived, this one from Captain Mosely who stated that his scouts had discovered the Indian army a short distance from Hatfield. Remembering how the Indians had decoyed the soldiers when they attacked Springfield, Appleton decided to go to Hatfield's aid. He first sent a messenger to Northampton to advise them of his plans, then raced to Hatfield, leaving only 20 men to guard Hadley.

THE NIPMUCKS UNSUCCESSFULLY ATTACK HATFIELD

Muttawmp attacked Hatfield on October 19 with a force of almost 800 warriors. He first built several huge fires a few miles from the town, hoping to create the impression that some houses were on fire, then positioned his men on both sides of the road leading to them. Just as he planned, the blazes created a sensation within the town, but neither Captain Mosely nor Captain Poole would risk any of their men to find out what was taking place.

When the fires continued to burn brightly, the settlers begged the two officers to investigate, fearing that some of their friends might be in need of help, but they remained adamant until noon, when Mosely at last agreed to send ten men to the fires. The men left almost immediately, and when they were securely in the trap, the Indians opened fire from both sides of the road, killing five of them, and wounding four others so seriously that they were easily captured. The last man in the column was more fortunate than his companions, for he wheeled his horse about when the first shots rang out, and galloped back to Deerfield closely followed by several Indians.

The fleeing soldier reached the safety of the town just as Major Appleton and his men arrived from the opposite direction. When Appleton saw the Indians approaching, he quickly ordered Mosely to guard the center of the town while he and Poole each guarded an end. The Indians gave up the chase when they saw the huge concentration of soldiers and returned to the camp where they reported to Muttawmp.

Even though Muttawmp now realized that he could not possibly take the town with the manpower available to him, he decided to go ahead with the attack, feeling that he could do enough damage to make the attempt worthwhile. He separated his men into three units, one of which he sent to the center of the town, and one at each end. The three mounted a simultaneous attack which was quickly repulsed, and they retreated out of gunshot range for awhile, then attacked again. They did this several more times, and although they managed to burn a number of houses and barns, they did very little other damage. Seeing that the town could not be taken, Muttawmp ordered his men to withdraw. They had captured several more soldiers throughout the day, and they were taken to their fort along with the first four prisoners.

THE WESTERN CAMPAIGN COMES TO A CLOSE

In a report to the Commissioners, Captain Samuel Appleton wrote that the Indians would soon be in their winter quarters. Since he did not anticipate any trouble from them during the winter months, he thought it would be wise to allow most of the soldiers to return to civilian life. This could be done without endangering the frontier towns if a small permanent garrison was left in each of them during the winter. Although he did not mention that his men were in a state of near mutiny, this was the case, and he was finding it increasingly difficult to maintain discipline. Major Treat was his biggest problem. He constantly threatened to return to Connecticut, and he remained where he was only because Appleton threatened to have him shot as a deserter if he tried to leave.

Appleton had as many problems with the settlers as he did with the soldiers, for most of them were sure they could not survive the winter, and they begged Appleton to provide them with an escort to any of the towns near the coast.

The exasperated Appleton would not supply the needed escort, and told them he would execute anyone who attempted to leave without his written permission. When he learned that several settlers had moved to Connecticut without notifying him first, he issued a proclamation in which he ordered that no one living in either Springfield, Hadley, Westfield, Northampton, or Hatfield "shall remove from or desert any of these towns ... nor shall any go out of the towns without a pass under the hand of the Commander-in-chief."

Appleton was unable to keep Major Treat at his post as he had hoped, for he received a number of letters from the Connecticut Council stating that they had received intelligence that the Indians were planning to attack the

Connecticut settlements in the winter. They needed Major Treat and his men to protect them, and demanded he be allowed to return. Disgusted with Connecticut's lack of cooperation, Appleton dismissed Treat and his men on November 19.

That same day, he wrote to Governor Leverett, complaining that the Commissioners had not yet answered his last letter, and explaining that he had allowed the Connecticut soldiers to return home. He said that his horses were so ill-fed that most of them were already unfit for service, while the cattle could not possibly survive the winter with the food supplies that were then available in the region.

Shortly after Governor Leverett received this letter, he learned that Philip was no longer in Massachusetts, but in Albany, where he expected to remain throughout the winter. This meant the colony would not have to maintain a full-time force in the west until spring, and he convinced the Commissioners to give Appleton permission to return home. When Appleton received this message, he first garrisoned the various river towns for the winter, leaving 39 men at Springfield, 29 at Westfield, 30 at Hadley, and 36 at Hatfield, then appointed a Council of War from among the leading men of these towns, and marched the rest of his men to Boston where they were discharged on November 25.

THE PATRIOT INDIANS IN THEIR WINTER QUARTERS

In November, as winter was closing in, most of the Nipmucks retired to their fortress near the base of Mount Wachusett where they planned to remain until spring. Because of their involvement in the war, they had raised and harvested only a small percentage of the food they would need to sustain them through the winter, but they were fortunate in that their war parties, continuing to raid the nearby settlements, still brought in large amounts of grain and a few head of cattle almost every day. This was accomplished with so little effort that Muttawmp, Shoshanim, and Monoco, all of whom were perennial optimists, were certain they would have no trouble feeding all their people until spring.

King Philip did not share their optimism, for he became uneasy when he saw how profligate the Indians were with their precious food. Neither was he particularly happy with the progress of the war to this time. He and Canonchet originally planned to mount such massive attacks against each of the frontier settlements that they would be completely destroyed before the end of summer. Once the inland areas were under Indian control, the combined patriot forces would march toward the sea, driving the English before them until they had no choice but to leave New England or face certain annihilation. Although Northfield and Deerfield had been evacuated, the other frontier towns were still intact, and were now so heavily garrisoned that they could be taken only if the Indians were willing to suffer heavy losses. He could not afford the luxury of a long, drawn-out war, for this would work to the advantage of the English. They had seemingly-inexhaustible supplies of food, guns, ammunition, and even manpower while the Indians had to exist on what they themselves produced, and could draw only from a pitifully small population to replace those warriors who were killed in combat or taken prisoner.

Only the Narragansetts of Rhode Island could supply the manpower and resources he needed to fight the war to a successful conclusion. They were not only the largest federation in New England in terms of population, but they harvested so much corn each year that they sold much of their surplus to the English. It is true that Canonchet had promised he would join in the war the following spring, but it was also true that there were many ways in which the English could pressure him into remaining neutral.

Philip was afraid that without the Narrgansetts on his side, he would also lose the Nipmucks, for most of them might defect when food became scarce in late winter. Therefore, during the first week in December, he left the village at Mount Wachusett, and travelled to Narragansett Country, hoping that his presence might encourage Canonchet to keep his promise.

**NEXT: THE GREAT SWAMP FIGHT, THE DEATH
OF PHILIP, AND THE END OF THE WAR**